A Mom's Life...in Status Updates

A Mom's Life...
In Status Updates

Christine Skluzacek

A Mom's Life...in Status Updates

© 2013 Christine Skluzacek
All rights reserved.

ISBN: 9781484125359

This book was printed in the United States of America.

To My Inspirations:
Landon, Luke, Connor and Evan

A Mom's Life...in Status Updates

"Chuckle along with this Minnesota mom as she chronicles her daily life through hilarious Facebook status updates. Enjoy the quirky quotes and oddball antics of a house filled with four boys."

A little bit about us...

Mom (Chris): Facebook junkie, lover of all things royal (mostly plastic crowns), Little House in the Prairie fan, forever "29".

Dad (Bruce): Man of many interests (beekeeping, snowkiting, woodworking, vineyard growing, excavating), fancy dresser, big talker.

Makayla (Kayla): My lovely stepdaughter who moved away to college before the true chaos began. Lucky girl.

Landon (Landy Pandy Puddin Pie): Math brain, video game master.

Luke (Connor's twin): Idolizes big brother Landon, perfectionist.

Connor (Luke's twin): Loves animals and broccoli, clown.

Evan (Evan Cutie Bird): baby of the family, smart, sassy, spoiled.

A Mom's Life...in Status Updates

T

-2009-

Landon: 6, Luke & Connor: 3, Evan: ½

April 23, 2009
It's a two beer night when one twin poops on the floor and the other one picks it up to show you.

June 5, 2009
It's amazing how many green beans a kid will eat if you pour Hershey's syrup over them.

July 3, 2009
I asked Landon to smell the flower and he said, "Mom, I can't smell it, my ears are plugged."

July 9, 2009
Landon: "Mom, you look kind of skinnier today."
Who said you can't have favorites?

July 20, 2009
Me: "Come boys let's go outside and have some fun!"
Boys playing their video games, "We hate fun."

July 21, 2009
Connor said he doesn't want to get a haircut because, "I don't want to run out of hair."

July 22, 2009
Landon asked me what I want to be when I grow up. I hope it's not too late to be a princess.

July 26, 2009
Why do I bother buying toys when 20 rolls of toilet paper will keep the kids busy for hours?

A Mom's Life...in Status Updates

July 28, 2009
I have given up on trying to stop the rough housing. Now I just tell them to "go fight in the other room."

August 8, 2009
Tonight we went out to eat and the boys ate all the sugar packets, jelly packets, ketchup and creamer. I think from now on I will only serve them condiments.

August 12, 2009
You know you live in a houseful of boys when all of the little figurines in your house are headless.

August 14, 2009
Why is it that I can never make it through a meal without having to go and wipe someone's butt?

August 27, 2009
Things I've said today:
"Keep your teeth to yourself!"
"Who put the tomato in the toilet??"

August 28, 2009
Unexpected bonus from a trip to the ER with Luke: I received a compliment from the doctor who said I was "well preserved" for having four kids.

August 29, 2009
Nothing like spending a perfect summer evening driving around town looking for a laxative suppository.

September 9, 2009
Brought four kids in to get their flu shots. Only succeeded with 3.

September 25, 2009
I found it's easiest to clean the 2 potty chairs by taking a shower with them. Not a pretty visual but effective.

September 27, 2009
Playing children's games at the church festival, Connor backed up and fell right into the duck pond. I tried really, really hard not to laugh.

September 28, 2009
Luke just found some holy water in the drawer and drank it. I'm wondering if it will help.

September 28, 2009
I always feel like a better mom when I make the fish sticks in the oven rather than the microwave. I think I will try this with chicken nuggets tomorrow.

September 30, 2009
Our daily discussion on the way to daycare, "Now boys, remember no fighting, no hitting, no pinching, no slapping, no kicking, no scratching, no poking, no wrestling, no grabbing, no flicking, no punching" and then Landon added, "and no snake bites."

October 3, 2009
It's a tad bit depressing when the highlight of my day is when a friend gives me a bag of used boy's underwear.

October 20, 2009
Evan got his first tooth today. Good for him. Bad for the breast.

October 21, 2009
I guess Connor wants a sister, "Mom, I think you should poop a girl out of your belly next time."

October 26, 2009
Today the twins were playing with their tools and actually dismantled part of the coffee table!

A Mom's Life...in Status Updates

October 28, 2009
The toothfairy forgot to put money under Landon's pillow last night. Luckily, I saved the day and found the money hiding under one of his stuffed animals.

November 2, 2009
I just witnessed a 20 minute tantrum because I flushed the toilet when a certain 3-year-old wanted to flush it himself.

November 3, 2009
Question of the day by Landon, "How do bad guys make you go blind?"

November 4, 2009
Talking about the different presidents and I mentioned Garfield. Landon was so shocked, "Garfield is a CAT. Our president was a CAT? Did we have any dogs?"

November 9, 2009
Landon said he can't watch the movie Happy Gilmore because it has "square words" in it.

November 15, 2009
If a three-year-old has himself locked in the bathroom and he says he is "cleaning up" it's best to mentally prepare yourself before opening the door.

November 17, 2009
Why must noise and chaos follow me where ever I go? And did I mention that I changed the twins' names to noise and chaos?

November 24, 2009
I just discovered that dusting has its advantages; I found 5 nerf bullets and a bag of Skittles!

November 24, 2009
I just got a call that I won a case of beer. Which is lucky because I'm thirsty.

November 25, 2009
It's nice that the twins are potty trained, but I'm not liking the fact that they think it's fun to pee everywhere; on the wall, in the garbage can, on each other.

November 29, 2009
For some reason I get nervous when I use the garbage disposal. I always think that something is going to fly out and impale me in the eye!

December 1, 2009
Connor came running out of the bathroom with a plunger on his head. Note: this is NOT a clean plunger.

December 16, 2009
Bruce is whining that he wishes he had longer arms so he wouldn't have to bend over to pick up stuff.

December 20, 2009
I'm contemplating if I would be considered a redneck if I give someone ammunition for a Christmas present.

December 21, 2009
Some kids sleep with soft, fluffy animals. Mine all sleep with hard, plastic tool boxes.

December 29, 2009
Every time I do the laundry I have to throw out at least 2 socks because of holes. At this rate we will be sockless by next Tuesday.

A Mom's Life...in Status Updates

-2010-

Landon: 7, Luke & Connor: 4, Evan: 1

January 4, 2010
I can't find my wedding ring or my mother's ring! So, does this mean I am no longer a wife or mom if I don't have rings to prove it?

January 9, 2010
We are all taking eye drops for pink eye and I spot Connor carrying around the super glue saying, "Mom, are these your eye drops?"

January 17, 2010
The kids got into, and destroyed the game closet. It looks like a tornado hit! So instead of being the good mom and sorting through all the pieces...it all went directly into the garbage. Yep, Mom of the year.

January 19, 2010
I tell Bruce over and over, "Power tools and kids are not a good combination."

January 19, 2010
The twins and I took a walk out to the mailbox and on the way they managed to drop every piece of mail on the ground, except for the credit card bill.

January 24, 2010
I feel like suing Wii Fit for harassment! It called me an overweight, uncoordinated 64 year old!

January 26, 2010
Connor got to choose supper tonight: apples, applesauce and cheese.

January 28, 2010
I'm feeling a little guilty that I bought a box of Fruity Pebbles (and hid it from the kids.)

February 1, 2010
Trying to get 10 short minutes on the computer, I found myself telling the boys, "Would you just go play, here play with the stapler."

February 7, 2010
Landon's quote of the day, "It's no fair, every Sunday church ruins our fun!"

February 13, 2010
The boys refer to their camouflage wallets as their "hunting purses."

February 14, 2010
I love going out to eat when three out of the four kids are FREE because they are 4 and under! One of the benefits of having so many kids!

February 23, 2010
I'm happy that Landon is learning how to read, but also annoyed because I can no longer skip half the words when I'm reading books.

February 25, 2010
Landon's questions of the day:
1. Who was the first person in jail?
2. Do boogers grow?
3. Do you wear clothes in heaven?

February 26, 2010
Loading the dishwasher and there among the dirty plates, bowls and cups is a pair of Scooby Doo underwear.

A Mom's Life...in Status Updates

February 27, 2010
We now have a "puke room" in our house. Unfortunately, it's my bedroom.

February 28, 2010
My day just wouldn't be complete without being sharted on.

March 1, 2010
Me: "Landon what do you think of my sweater?"
Landon: "It's ok. I'm kind of wondering where Fat Albert buys his clothes."

March 2, 2010
Connor: "Mom, Luke jumped on me and wiggled my heart!"

March 15, 2010
Landon informed me that he no longer wants to be an astronaut; he now wants to be a truck driver.

March 16, 2010
I'm filling out my 2010 US Census. I can't wait to find out how many people are living in this house!

March 19, 2010
This should be interesting; reps from the Supernanny are coming over on Sunday to see the kids. Let the fighting begin!

March 20, 2010
We had "Cops" on TV and Luke pointed to a toothless, strung out woman and he said, "Mom she looks like you."

March 29, 2010
Did you know that when M&Ms go through the washing machine the coating comes off and they look like little chocolate bunny turds?

March 30, 2010
Every time Connor calls me a "beautiful princess" I can't help but like him a little bit more.

March 30, 2010
I'm pretty sure that if I had to, I could survive on chocolate and nacho cheese.

March 31, 2010
While packing my suitcase, Luke decided to put superglue all over the desk and his hands. I suddenly don't feel too guilty about going to Europe for 10 days.

April 13, 2010
There is nothing quite as disgusting as a ziplock bag full of 11 days of dirty socks and underwear!!

April 15, 2010
4 boys in the tub = 75% of the water out of the tub.

April 16, 2010
Someone mentioned that my baby Evan looks like "Shrek." I'm not sure if I should laugh or cry.

April 20, 2010
I thought I would be nice and let Evan run around free (without a diaper) after his bath. It backfired, he peed on my pillow.

April 21, 2010
We have a new contest going at our house. Tick-a-palooza!! The one with the most ticks wins!! The winner will get a candy bar or Lyme disease.

April 22, 2010
Landon yelled across the yard, "Hey Mom...can you put my nuts in your pocket?" He should have said "acorns" but that wouldn't have been as funny.

A Mom's Life...in Status Updates

April 25, 2010
I have discovered that our house is divided into 2 camps: those who like grape jelly and those who like strawberry. (p.s. grape rules!)

April 25, 2010
Tick update: Evan and I are holding at 1, Connor and Landon are at 3, Luke is creeping up there with 5 and Bruce is leading the pack with 8. He is and always will be a tick magnet.

May 4, 2010
The kids were helping bake banana bread. It went well until Luke licked the baking powder and proceeded to spit it out into the batter.

May 6, 2010
There was a tick floating in the bathtub and the boys were all fighting over who gets to claim it.

May 8, 2010
For some reason some of my kids don't like it when I call them by their nicknames: Evan Cutie Bird, Lukey Love, Connor Bear and Landy Pandy Puddin' Pie.

May 17, 2010
I wonder if a screwdriver is considered a dangerous weapon because Luke went to preschool with one in his pocket.

May 18, 2013
The toothfairy didn't come last night. It must have been too windy for her to travel.

May 19, 2010
The twins couldn't stop talking about the fire drill they had at school. "First we had to go OUTSIDE and then we went back INSIDE!"

May 21, 2010
A little word of wisdom: If a 4 year old boy asks you to smell his finger, although it may be tempting, do NOT do it!

May 23, 2010
I'm hoping that "my son has purple permanent marker all over his face" is a valid excuse for missing church.

May 31, 2010
At supper I asked Connor not to wipe his face on his shirt. Instead he lifted his foot up and wiped his mouth with his sock.

June 3, 2010
I changed Landon's computer password to a "Presidents name." He's tried Obama and Lincoln so far. It might take him all summer to figure out it's Polk.

June 5, 2010
Connor had to pee outside so he went behind the shed and Evan followed him. When they came back a minute later, Evan's head was wet.

June 8, 2010
The twins wanted some more cookies so I asked them to say the magic word. They thought for a second and then Luke said, "elephant?" and Connor said, "house?"

June 9, 2010
We drove by a fancy coach bus and I asked Landon if that was his school bus. He laughed and said, "No Mom, don't you know that bus is only for Rock Stars!"

June 11, 2010
I have broken the most important motherhood commandment:
Thou shall not run out of ketchup.

A Mom's Life...in Status Updates

June 11, 2010
Spill the milk, no problem...spill the juice, things happen...spill my beer, that's a time-out mister!!

June 12, 2010
I'm totally willing to hire a professional sock-matcher upper.

June 15, 2010
FYI - ticks like belly buttons.

June 17, 2010
That storm warning wasted two hours of my life. Trying to keep everyone in the basement and entertained without electricity is worse than an actual tornado.

June 20, 2010
Connor just informed me that when he grows up he wants to have a mustache!
1. why?
2. noooooo!

June 20, 2010
I pretty much traumatized the kids with all my yelling, screaming and wacky ballet dancing when I spotted a snake in the garden.

June 22, 2010
At the restaurant Evan was throwing fries and wiping pudding in his hair. Landon commented, "I really miss the good old days when Evan was a good boy."

June 24, 2010
A wise woman once told me that as a mother you will love all of your children equally but differently. I definitely have one boy on the "different" side tonight!

June 28, 2010
On my first try giving the boys haircuts, two are lopsided, one is almost bald and the smart one ran away.

June 28, 2010
Landon likes math and said, "Hey mom, in 2 years you will be fo..." I stopped him and said, "Don't you EVER say the F word again!"

June 28, 2010
Darn kids are staying up too late and are seriously cutting into my "me" time!!

June 29, 2010
Evan went down in the basement and then came up with only his diaper and a cowboy hat on. What kind of wild parties are they having down there? And why wasn't I invited?

July 3, 2010
Happy quote of the day by Connor, "Mom, I like your face."

July 5, 2010
Saw another snake in the garden, but this time Bruce and the boys picked it up, petted it and released it into the wild. Hello...we have a SHOVEL...use it!

July 9, 2010
I just found myself laughing out loud hysterically while watching Curious George. Yes, my mind has turned into mush but that little monkey is funny!

July 10, 2010
One nice thing about living in the country is that you can go outside and pants are optional.

A Mom's Life...in Status Updates

July 16, 2010
Why is it that within 10 minutes of arriving at a wedding reception a child spills a whole kiddie cocktail on his white shirt? Seriously, I can drink 10 beers and not spill anything!

July 17, 2010
The boys have taken to using fresh produce as weapons. I would have never imagined that zucchini could be used as swords.

July 24, 2010
Two big trees are down from the storm last night. It's times like this that I'm happy that I'm not trusted to use a chainsaw.

July 25, 2010
We went to see "The Corpse Flower- the stinkiest in the world." I think it smells better than the interior of my van.

July 25, 2010
Connor: "I forgot to brush my teeth so I cleaned them with my spit."

July 25, 2010
Connor: "If I was on the Titanic and it started to sink I would just sit on the iceberg and drink coffee."

July 25, 2010
Landon: "Church would be more fun if it had a lot less talking."

July 26, 2010
Luke's not so bright idea of the day, "Let's have a tug of war with our teeth."

July 26, 2010
Landon was being greedy with the candy at the parade and I asked him, "Why do you always want everything you see?"
Landon: "Well, so do you!"
Me: "Like what?"
Landon: "A husband."

July 27, 2010
I was the crazy mom at Walmart yelling at the kids: "Would everyone just grab your balls and get in!!" (meaning: please pick up your bouncy balls and kindly get into the cart, thank you sweet children of mine.)

July 30, 2010
I'm trying to give myself a "time out" but it's not working, everyone keeps following me around.

July 31, 2010
My van became even messier when a HUGE carton of goldfish crackers poured out all over the back seat. I'm going to leave it there. Built in snacks.

August 2, 2010
Seriously, what part of "courtesy flush" don't you understand?

August 3, 2010
My stepdaughter, Makayla, said that I'm the weirdest person she knows. Oddly enough, I take that as a compliment!

August 4, 2010
I get kind of sad when I see a semi-truck full of chickens driving down the road. And it's even worse when I have to tell the kids that they are going to the zoo.

A Mom's Life...in Status Updates

August 8, 2010
After getting all of the school supplies organized I found Connor under the table using a glue stick like chapstick.

August 9, 2010
I tried explaining to the twins that part of swimming lessons is actually getting INTO the pool.

August 12, 2010
Only when I'm at Subway, when another car pulls in the same time I do, I run like a crazy woman to beat them in line.

August 15, 2010
I love church festivals. When else can you grab a beer right after you get out of church?

August 17, 2010
This morning Luke said, "Mom, your breath is as smelly as the stinkiest flower in the world" and then brought me a toothbrush.

August 23, 2010
Kids have a different view of the world. Landon, "China is really, really nice. They make lots of stuff for us."

August 24, 2010
I learned a new trick. If the kids say "ick, I don't like that" for supper, I go in the corner, wrap up said food in a tortilla shell with cheese and suddenly they like it.

September 1, 2010
Sometimes it sounds like everyone in this house has a megaphone attached to their mouth.

September 3, 2010
I overheard Connor tell Luke, "Don't walk on the floor, mommy mopped it. Isn't that weird?"

September 3, 2010
I told the kids they could each pick out 2 things at the dollar store and ended up spending $32. How did my kids multiply while we were in the store?

September 6, 2010
The boys showed me that if you put a bike tire pump nozzle in the toilet and pump it, it will make cool bubbles.

September 10, 2010
Things I want to invent: seatbelts that kids can't take off, TV remotes that don't get lost and beer that has no calories.

September 14, 2010
Luke was digging through the dirty laundry pile looking for his pants. He said he wanted to find the frog he put in his pocket.

September 20, 2010
It takes a long time to get anywhere when you have to stop the van three times to buckle up 2 four year olds!!

September 21, 2010
Connor was eating some chocolate chips, smiled and said, "These make me happy." I know exactly how he feels!

September 24, 2010
The first place that Landon would like to visit is China because, "I really like the China buffet."

September 26, 2010
Someone in this family just had a major meltdown because I wouldn't let him sleep with a bag of gummy worms.

October 3, 2010
I asked Connor what his name was and he said, "Connor."
I asked him what his last name is and he said, "Luke."

A Mom's Life...in Status Updates

October 6, 2010
We had our family pictures taken this afternoon. Besides the bloody nose, the bloody lip, and the crabby toddler, I think it went well.

October 7, 2010
I've resorted to asking the kids, "Would Jesus take off his seatbelt?" According to them, he would.

October 8, 2010
The twins didn't want to play with the new boy at daycare. When asked why Luke said, "Because he smelled like chicken."

October 16, 2010
Grandma was over visiting and when she went to the bathroom, Landon whispered, "I wonder if she going 1 or 2?"

October 25, 2010
I asked Landon how the twins were on the bus and he replied, "Not good, Luke licked his library book all the way home."

November 1, 2010
Quote of the day by Landon, "It's hard to talk and think at the same time."

November 2, 2010
I was putting food down the garbage disposal and Connor asked me if I was feeding a monster.

November 6, 2010
Lesson for the day: If you see a matchbox car in the toilet, don't just flush it and hope it goes down.

November 9, 2010
For a brief second I considered trading a kid for a Kirby vacuum cleaner.

November 11, 2010
Landon is down to his last pair of uniform pants. So every day after school I have to chase him around the house demanding he take his pants off.

November 13, 2010
In the time it took me to take a shower, the boys dragged up our 13 foot Christmas tree from the basement.

November 16, 2010
Taco salad for supper, but someone thought it needed another ingredient and added a bag of chocolate chips.

November 26, 2010
Offered to pay Landon 5 cents a pair for matching up socks. He earned $3.15. (Yes, that is 63 pairs of socks.) Best money I ever spent!

November 29, 2010
Connor drew a picture of a person on the wall next to his bed. Now he says, "I can't sleep, that guy is looking at me."

November 30, 2010
Landon told me that he is going to be an astronaut and if I was "still alive" he would bring me a rock from mars.

December 1, 2010
We were writing our letters to Santa and Connor asked for a big gun and a computer without e-mail or passwords, only games.

December 2, 2010
Two words that you don't want to hear coming from the bathroom, "pee fight."

December 12, 2010
I'm happy this blizzard is over and I can go to work tomorrow. Family time is good, as long as it's in moderation.

A Mom's Life...in Status Updates

December 13, 2010
Landon: "Dad + kids = fun and Mom + kids = love"
Me: "So what does kids + kids = ?"
Landon: "Trouble!"

December 15, 2010
I put on some red lipstick and Connor asked, "Mom, why do you have angry lips?"

December 17, 2010
You know it's the Christmas season when you are on a first name basis with the guy in the electronics section at Target.

December 20, 2010
There was a really old, gray haired grandpa on TV and Landon said, "Dad, that's what you will look tomorrow."

December 21, 2010
Sounds like there is some redecorating going on, I heard Luke tell Connor, "Help me move this couch or I won't be your best friend."

December 25, 2010
I guess Santa was feeling extra generous, even the kids on the naughty list got presents this year.

December 28, 2010
It's sad when the most exercise I get is wrestling my kids to a timeout.

December 29, 2010
Connor: "So how long do I have to be me?"
Mom: "Forever, why? Who do you want to be?"
Connor: "Luke."

December 29, 2010
I have learned something very disturbing about my husband. He calls a "spatula" a "rubber scraper." So wrong.

-2011-

Landon, 8; Luke & Connor, 5; Evan, 2

January 5, 2011
After I clipped Connor's fingernails, he picked up a clipping, looked at it and said, "This is my best friend."
Then he ate it.

January 7, 2011
The bad news: I overslept by 2 hours this morning. The good news: it's the first time I've gotten 8 hours of sleep in nine years!

January 8, 2011
Why is it that although this house is thousands of square feet, yet someone always has to be within 2 inches of me?

January 8, 2011
You know the outcome is not going to be good when you hear: "I'm gonna hammer you."
"Oh yeah, I'm gonna scissors you."

January 14, 2011
What's the first thing a group of 8-year-old boys do at a birthday party? Handcuff a sock monkey to the dining room light.

January 17, 2011
A day doesn't go by that I don't get mooned.

January 17, 2011
I told Landon that I have to remember to give him his birthday spankings and he said, "Oh mom, you won't remember, you will be thinking of other things like ponies and rainbows."

A Mom's Life...in Status Updates

January 19, 2011
There is a tooth mark in my deodorant. I wonder who has powder fresh breath this morning.

January 19, 2011
I was checking out a strange mole on the back of Landon's neck and got kind of worried. I turned on the light for a closer look. It was a booger.

January 20, 2011
I don't really care for days that involve bodily functions which require paper towels and Lysol.

January 21, 2011
I sent President Obama a Christmas card and invited him over for spaghetti supper. The White House called today and said they reviewed my request but he is unable to come because of security reasons. (He must have gotten wind about the Skluzacek boys.)

January 22, 2011
Today I learned that it's hard to eat lunch while wearing toy handcuffs.

January 26, 2011
Gone are the days when I could put all four boys in the tub at once. Now it has to be done in shifts...cleanest to dirtiest.

January 29, 2011
I may have spent a majority of my morning dreaming of a Swiss boarding school.

January 31, 2011
Connor: "Mom, I found a mouse in the basement, but it was stinky so I threw it in the garbage."

January 31, 2011
Bruce discovered that the mouse was actually a shrew. Then I overheard Luke tell Connor, "Your hair smells like a shrew."

February 1, 2011
Beware of quiet children, they may be in the bathroom dipping the toilet brush in the toilet and washing the walls with it.

February 1, 2011
I have an old antique wooden phone hanging in the office. Landon looked at it and asked, "Mom, why do you have that old phone from the 1990s?"

February 2, 2011
Even a standard run-of-the-mill pillow fight results in a head injury at our house.

February 3, 2011
Getting everything ready for taxes tomorrow and realize one benefit of having lots of kids, tax deductions!

February 4, 2011
What happens when your husband complains that you have too many coats? Buy three more coats.

February 7, 2011
I'm wondering if it's too late for me to join a convent.

February 9, 2011
I put an "educational" DVD in our vehicle for the kids to watch and now I feel like the best mom ever.

February 9, 2011
Interesting quote of the day by Connor, "I want to beat up Santa and he will say, "HoHoHo I like it."

A Mom's Life...in Status Updates

February 11, 2011
I was not expecting this visual: A naked two year old running around the house, wiping his butt with my makeup brush.

February 13, 2011
Landon has a fever today and he was looking sad and said, "It's all my fault I'm sick. It's because I played the DS too long."

February 15, 2011
Random conversation at the Skluzacek house.
Me: "Connor, what do you want to do when you grow up?"
Connor: "Eat a wall"
Me: "I bet that would taste pretty gross."
Connor: "Tastes like chicken."

February 18, 2011
I brought the boys home some "special" gifts from Chicago: bags of airline peanuts and Oprah postcards.

February 21, 2011
I'm thinking that being outside stuck in a snow bank would be better than listening to all the commotion going on in this house.

February 22, 2011
I was listening to the twins talk after I put them to bed and Luke whispered, "Connor is a stinky butt and a loser, Amen."

February 27, 2011
For a special treat I bought Neapolitan ice cream and when Landon looked at the colors he said, "Wow, is this real or is it a dream?"

March 8, 2011
Landon's random question of the day, "So, what's so circus-y about a clown car?"

March 10, 2011
Nothing wrecks your Burger King experience more than the kid at the next table puking all over the floor.

March 10, 2011
Connor bumped his head and I asked Bruce to get me an icepack. He handed me a bag of frozen breast milk.

March 11, 2011
Shopping for a first communion outfit and Landon said, "I want to wear something with more KA-ZAZ. You know, like a tuxedo."

March 12, 2011
For Landon's homework, he had to describe himself using the letters of his name. I had to laugh when I read it:
L- Likes animals
A- A good friend
N- Nose picker

March 16, 2011
Planning my to do list for when I win the lottery:
1. hire a nanny
...that's about it

March 17, 2011
No complaints about the kids today. But I did have to put some meatloaf in Bruce's shoe to teach him a lesson.

March 19, 2011
The twins were very excited to show me something "really cool." They drew pictures on the bathroom windows with my deodorant! Cool.

A Mom's Life...in Status Updates

March 20, 2011
I can't even escape to the bathroom for one minute before Luke is knocking on the door, "Please can I come in? I promise I won't laugh."

March 24, 2011
Me: "Ok boys, where is my broom?"
Landon: "I don't know, the last time I saw it I was hitting Luke with it."

March 27, 2011
Landon: "I was wondering, what's the definition of wine? Is it beer?"

March 28, 2011
You know you're a redneck when: You see a deer in the backyard and your son gets his toy gun to shoot it.

March 31, 2011
I walk into the kitchen and one child is drinking maple syrup, one is shaking salt on the floor and one is swinging from the microwave door. Who are these people and why must they destroy my home?

April 2, 2011
I signed up the boys for Karate. I figured if they are going to fight they might as well fight ninja style!

April 3, 2011
My McDonalds order, "1 parfait, 2 McChicken, 7 double cheeseburgers, 6 fries, and 1 McBarf Bag."

April 5, 2011
Receptionist on the phone: "May I tell them who is calling?"
Me: "Chris Skluzacek"
Receptionist: "Kristin Potcheck"
Me: "Um, yah."

April 7, 2011
It was a mistake letting Luke sleep with us. He gave me minute to minute updates of the time. "Mom, it's 11:23....11:24....11:25" and on and on.

April 8, 2011
There is nothing worse than going to put your kids to bed and then realizing that all of their bedding is still in the washing machine.

April 11, 2011
I had to tell my dentist a little confession today. I really would have flossed my teeth but my boys used all of the floss to decorate the house.

April 15, 2011
Landon was sad saying, "No girls in my class like me."
I told him, "Oh, I'm sure some of them like you!"
He said, "No, they don't. I asked all of them."

April 17, 2011
Landon went to a radio station with Kayla and then informed me, "Mom, at the radio station he just presses buttons, there is not a real band there."

April 19, 2011
Two words you don't want to hear coming from the bedroom, "booger war."

April 20, 2011
Luke knows how to spell 2 words. Luke and poop.

April 22, 2011
Beware of a quiet 2 year old, he may be in the bathroom organizing your feminine hygiene supplies by size, color and function.

A Mom's Life...in Status Updates

April 23, 2011
Coloring Easter eggs is always a traumatic experience. Spilling dye everywhere, having a fit, breaking eggs and that's just me.

April 24, 2011
Landon: "Mom, tell me the truth, is Santa the Easter Bunny?"

April 27, 2011
Quote of the day, "Mom, I see a problem. There is a dead deer in our living room."

April 27, 2011
Why is it that I leave the room for a minute and when I come back someone is licking my toast?

April 30, 2011
Connor picked me the first dandelion of the season which I now proudly display in a cup on the counter... until no one is looking, and then it will magically disappear.

April 30, 2011
A day just isn't complete without a call to the Poison Control Center from the frozen food isle of Walmart.

May 1, 2011
Landon had his first communion this morning. The kids were all so cute in their ties and white dresses and Luke whispered to me, "Is Landon getting married?"

May 2, 2011
I took Connor grocery shopping and asked him to help me find some celery for a salad I was making and he said, "Ok. But mom, what's celery?"

May 5, 2011
Who needs toys? The most popular thing at our house is a hunk of Styrofoam that they call, "The Hand of Doom.

May 6, 2011
I thought I would try to clean the toaster since one side didn't want to work anymore. When I shook it upside down....a set of keys fell out. That explains it.

May 8, 2011
I woke up with 4 boys trying to snuggle and kiss me all at the same time, but then a fight broke out. Happy Mother's Day.

May 9, 2011
Luke told auntie Laura, "You look really, really handsome!"

May 11, 2011
For mother's day I bought myself a very special gift, a Life Commemorative Edition of the Royal Wedding. And wouldn't you know it someone spilled water on it already. I've decided when I buy something for myself I will just throw it directly in the garbage to save time.

May 14, 2011
There once was a beautiful, young mother, wearing a crown, who threatened her young son with flatulence if he didn't let go of her leg. It worked.

May 15, 2011
The boys just started a "Brothers Bike Club." Watch out Hell's Angels!

May 19, 2011
Tomorrow is our 11th wedding anniversary and I think I will surprise Bruce with the best present ever, staying married to him.

May 20, 2011
Landon: "Mom, you have to butter my toast because if I do it, it won't taste as good."

A Mom's Life...in Status Updates

May 20, 2011
Waiting for some guy from Craig's list to come and look at our pool. I plan on telling him, "my professional wrestler, ex-marine, navy seal sharp shooter, mobster husband should be home any minute now."

May 22, 2011
Confession: Before throwing away an old guitar today, I smashed it like a rock star.

May 24, 2011
I am mortified. This morning on the way to work, Bruce noticed an elderly lady, about 85, in her yard, carrying around a leaf blower cleaning her lawn. He had to look twice because she was wearing the same pajamas that I have!

May 26, 2011
I asked 2-year-old Evan, "Where is your shoe?" and he points to his mouth and laughs. Wonder what that means.

May 26, 2011
I asked Landon if he wanted more taco salad and he said, "No thanks. It feels like it's coming up through my nose."

May 27, 2011
Sitting on the toilet, Connor yells, "Hey mom, there's chocolate frosting on the wall." That's not frosting.

May 28, 2011
Connor: "Mom, if you were a girl, I'd marry you."

June 3, 2011
I introduced the boys to the sandwich I grew up on: the peanut butter, jelly and potato chip sandwich. They didn't like it, food snobs.

June 6, 2011
I discovered a benefit of having a pool…less baths!

June 7, 2011
It's too hot for cooking, so its Subway sandwiches for lunch and then Subway crumbs for supper.

June 9, 2011
Landon: "Mom, I think I forgot to put on underwear today."

June 12, 2011
It's pretty hard to answer the phone when your son locks you out of the house.

June 13, 2011
Landon: "Mom, do you like losing $80?"
Me: "No"
Landon: "Well, that's how much you lost when you bought four pillow pets."

June 18, 2011
It never fails, whenever there is a thunderstorm, you will find Bruce outside cleaning out the gutters.

June 18, 2011
The twins were fighting over a piece of cheese and Connor's argument was, "But I've loved this cheese since I was born!"

June 20, 2011
I'm pretty sure we've exceeded our hotdog limit for the week and it's only Monday.

June 20, 2011
Trying to get Connor in a time out and he informed me, "Jesus said I don't need a time out."

June 23, 2011
Quote of the day, "Get your stinky toes out of my corn!!"

A Mom's Life...in Status Updates

June 24, 2011
Too bad I really like my husband because sometimes I could go for every other weekend off from the kids.

June 26, 2011
I was reading a diet book and Landon said, "Mom, you're fine, just a little above average."

June 29, 2011
I've discovered that a life without carbs is a really, really sucky life!

July 1, 2011
I was putting the solar cover on the pool and a frog jumped in my face. I wonder if that was my prince.

July 2, 2011
Evan went potty all by himself (a first) and then he threw a new roll of toilet paper in the toilet (not a first).

July 3, 2011
Went out for lunch and the boys discovered how to make milk bubbles with their straws. It kept them entertained for a while, until the milk overfloweth and mommy got madeth.

July 7, 2011
Dad bought the boys spray candy and wouldn't you know it, Connor sprayed it up his nose. Apparently it stings.

July 8, 2011
If a dirty kitchen sink was a crime I would be on death row.

July 9, 2011
Evan was carrying around my cellphone outside and suddenly it was missing. We asked him where it was and he showed us. It was in the tail pipe of Bruce's truck.

July 11, 2011
Some days I feel oddly connected to the Octomom.

July 12, 2011
There is nothing worse than being all comfy and snuggled into bed when your eyes pop open. Toothfairy!

July 12, 2011
Luke now thinks he is Indiana Jones and is begging me to buy him a REAL whip. I'm kind of thinking this would be a bad idea.

July 19, 2011
Do other kids just randomly fall off of their stools when eating, or is it just mine?

July 20, 2011
Video games or sanity? That is the question.

July 17, 2011
Topic of the day: Heaven.
"Do we take a plane to get there? Are there moms in heaven? Who will get us food? What if we get thirsty, is there water? Are there computers in heaven and do the computers have passwords? What if we don't know the password?"

July 21, 2011
So my dad bought me 10 kids tickets for the circus. He must:
1. have forgotten how many kids I have
2. think I need a little more chaos in my life
3. really wants me to throw myself in the lion's cage

July 24, 2011
It's so weird, sitting in church, Landon whispers something to me and he has wine breath!

July 25, 2011
Connor: "I was really good today. I'm good every day now. I don't know what's happening to me."

A Mom's Life...in Status Updates

July 26, 2011
Thank you Evan for cleaning the mirror, with my toothbrush.

July 27, 2011
Only a mom would be searching the internet at midnight for a website on how to draw a pig.

July 28, 2011
Landon: "Mom, why can't we play the Wii? It's the Wii-kend!"

July 28, 2011
Connor lost another tooth and I asked him, "Guess who is coming over tonight with a beautiful dress, wings, a magic wand and a purse full of money?"
Connor: "Kayla!"

July 29, 2011
Landon loaded the dishwasher and he was so grossed out that he put on oven mitts to handle the plates and asked, "How can you do this every day?"

July 31, 2011
The kids won't eat spaghetti, but they will eat "bloody worm stew."

July 31, 2011
Connor: "When I go to heaven will I still pick my nose?"

August 1, 2011
Every day it's the same thing: Bruce complains that I have too many shampoo and conditioner bottles in the shower and then I complain that we need a bigger shower for all my hair products.

August 3, 2011
Me: "Connor why were you naughty at daycare?"
Connor: "Cuz I'm made of grass."

August 3, 2011
Twins in the tub, "Mom, help! Evan threw the toilet brush in the tub." Yet another reason why going in the pool should count as a taking a bath.

August 5, 2011
For his first stay at a hotel Landon packed: 3 stuffed animals, a twirly straw, a night light, holy water, and an 8x10 picture of himself.

August 8, 2011
Spending 3 days in Nebraska is 2 1/2 days too long.

August 9, 2011
After spending 7 hours in the car I have learned two important lessons:
1. Do not speak unless spoken to
2. Flatulence is frowned upon

July 31, 2011
A sure sign that it's time to do the dishes, when the kids have to use measuring cups for their drinks.

August 14, 2011
I'm not sure how I feel about getting a thank you card from a high school graduate that says, "Thanks for the money, I will be putting it towards my truck and a gun."

August 17, 2011
School bags are all packed and ready by the door. Now we are just waiting for the bus to come, dreaming of that big yellow hunk of salvation coming down the road to save me!

August 17, 2011
I must have been in some weird alternative universe when I thought it would be a "good idea" to buy each of the boys their own fly swatter.

A Mom's Life...in Status Updates

August 18, 2011

Landon's question of the day, "I don't get it, why do ladies in movies lay around with pickles in their eyes?"

August 18, 2011

Landon: "How old do you have to be to drive a car?"
Me: "16"
Landon: "How old do you have to be to drive a rocket?"

August 19, 2011

Landon is wearing a t-shirt that says, "I'm on a mission to annoy you." Mission accomplished.

August 21, 2011

Cleaning up the house and Bruce threatened to burn any toys that aren't picked up. Landon said, "Well fine, we'll burn your stuff, like your shoes and your website."

August 21, 2011

Labeling some things for school and Evan decided to label his feet, his legs and the couch with a permanent black marker.

August 24, 2011

This made me smile. Connor, "Mom, you look so beautiful; I want to kiss you all day."

August 25, 2011

Luke: "Mom, your breath smells like rotten banana juice."

August 26, 2011

When I read the ad in the paper to "host a foreign exchange student" I thought for a second, FREE NANNY! But then I figured it would not be good for international relations.

August 26, 2011
Luke: "Mom, what are those cows doing?"
Me: "I think they are trying to play leapfrog."

August 28, 2011
Embarrassing moment of the day, at Walmart a man approached me, "Excuse me ma'am, but you're leaking," as he points to the ground. (My milk jug sprung a leak.)

August 29, 2011
Another reason why you can't take your eyes off of a 2-year-old; your cell phone may end up in a cup of apple juice.

August 30, 2011
My husband called with an unusual request, "When I get home, I need you to help me unload a goat treadmill."

August 30, 2011
Connor: "Mom, if I pick my nose will I grow a mustache?"

August 31, 2011
Connor: "Mom, look at my beautiful drawing. It's a picture of a waterfall and a dead guy."

September 1, 2011
I was trying to teach the boys how to play hopscotch and Luke asked, "What's hopscotch? Is it like hotmama?"

September 3, 2011
What does it mean when a child says, "Mom, I pooped but I didn't wipe it on the wall." He wiped it on the wall.

September 3, 2011
The twins had a lot of questions about seeing a cow being butchered today. They wondered why do we eat cows and not people. I said we don't eat humans. Then Luke asked, "Oh, so do we eat cops?"

A Mom's Life...in Status Updates

September 4, 2011
What a night: 3 pukers and 1 diarrhea-er.

September 4, 2011
Kayla started college today and I dreamed of moving in the dorm with her! But no, I'm back home, eating popcorn and drinking beer. And all the boys around here are running around in their underwear, yelling and falling over...so I guess it's kind of like the dorm anyway.

September 5, 2011
Sure, I buy Landon a robe and now he walks around the house like he's Hugh Hefner.

September 6, 2011
Landon would make a great quarterback; he can throw a shoe across three rooms and hit Connor in the temple.

September 6, 2011
The boys were searching for a frog but had to settle for a new pet grasshopper that they named "Josh."

September 7, 2011
"I bet the toothfairy couldn't come last night because once a year she has to get her wings tuned up."

September 11, 2011
Landon: "Mom, you know how everyone has a special gift from God? Well, I think mine is beat boxing."

September 12, 2011
Evan pulled out an empty beer can from the garbage, handed it to me and said, "Mom, here's your coffee."

September 13, 2011
Connor has the stomach flu and is whining, "I don't want to go the hospital and see the dentist."

September 15, 2011
A word of advice: It is wise to look inside your oven before you turn it on as it may be a parking garage for matchbox cars.

September 18, 2011
I was trying to do a little meditation by taking deep breaths and Luke told me, "Mom, don't do that you're wasting all the air!

September 20, 2011
Landon: "Mom, I figured out why we are Czech: Sklu-za-check!"

September 21, 2011
Connor: "Mom, Luke licked Landon's lava lamp."

September 22, 2011
I had to inform the twins that they are now old enough to wear pants with zippers and buttons. Luke reluctantly agreed and Connor decided that he will no longer wear pants.

September 23, 2011
Landon: "Mom, did you and dad build this house out in the country so you can have lots of free parking spaces?"

September 24, 2011
Does spraying the bathrooms with Lysol and closing all closet doors count as cleaning? If so, mission accomplished!

September 24, 2011
I'm making supper and Landon yells from the bathtub, "Mom can you deliver my supper up here?"

September 25, 2011
I just got done showing the boys how to use a fire extinguisher. I'm pretty sure I will regret doing this.

A Mom's Life...in Status Updates

September 25, 2011
In church, Connor pulls a big hairy caterpillar out of his pocket and proudly shows it to everyone as we go up for communion.

September 27, 2011
Nappy time is Happy time.

September 28, 2011
I discovered that the kids don't like it when I brush their teeth when I have a "mad face."

September 29, 2011
I was yelling at the boys to finish their homework and Landon says, "Mom, you really look good in those shoes."

October 1, 2011
The twins were playing with matchbox cars and I overheard Luke say, "There aren't any seatbelts in these things. Are they trying to kill us?"

October 5, 2011
Connor looked sad and I asked him what was wrong and he said, "I don't want to be the band-aid boy or the nose-picking guy anymore."

October 7, 2011
Friday fun night activity: playing keep-away with Bruce's dirty sock. It's really fun until someone dry heaves.

October 9, 2011
80 fingernails and toenails cut...let the week begin.

October 12, 2011
There is nothing more annoying than a 2 cup coffee maker.

October 13, 2011
While shopping, the boys discovered that when you spin the sunglasses holder around really, really fast…ALL the glasses will fly off.

October 13, 2011
Lesson learned today: Perkins employees frown upon kids licking the pie case.

October 14, 2011
The guy next to me at the gas station was cleaning a tiny spot off of his Corvette. When I look at my dirty vehicle I see "LANDON" written in the dust across the whole side.

October 15, 2011
I have everyone in this house figured out. When Connor is quiet, he's sneaking snacks. When Luke is quiet, he's hiding from me. When Landon is quiet, he's sulking. When Evan is quiet, he's pooping. When Bruce is quiet, he's infecting our computer with viruses.

October 16, 2011
Took the family out to eat after church and when the twins came out of the restroom Luke yelled to everyone in the restaurant, "Connor has the diarrhea!"

October 16, 2011
It's kind of annoying when you go to use the salt shaker and nothing comes out because someone has licked it shut.

October 19, 2011
Connor informed me that he wants to bring the dead raccoon at the end of our driveway for show and tell.

October 22, 2011
I'm going to take ONE room in this house and claim it as my own. But first I need a deadbolt lock, an electric fence and a guard dog.

A Mom's Life...in Status Updates

October 22, 2011
Observation of the day: Connor dunks his Cheez-Its in milk.

October 23, 2011
The boys just invented a "ladybug launcher" out of an old hairclip. I think this just may be our million dollar idea.

October 24, 2011
I learn something new about my kids every day. Luke just informed me that he is allergic to unicorns.

October 25, 2011
Not so proud mommy moment of the day: I told the twins that I would give them candy for breakfast if they wore "zipper" pants to school. It worked.

October 27, 2011
Landon: "Do you think I will marry a pretty or ugly girl??"
Me: "What do you think?"
Landon: "Ugly."

October 28, 2011
Connor: "Luke your breath smells good, what's in your mouth?"
Luke: "Chocolate, fruit roll up and gum."

October 31, 2011
Landon was so proud and excited to present me with a gift. It was an elastic hair band he found in the parking lot of Kwik Trip.

October 31, 2011
Things you don't want your kids to say when trick-or-treating:
"I HATE licorice, what else do you have?"
"You're OLD!"
"I can spell my name, so can I have extra candy?"
"It smells like poop in there."

November 1, 2011
At the Kindergarten Halloween party, the pressure was on Connor to throw the beanbag in the ghost's mouth. The room was silent as everyone waited in anticipation. Then Connor farts. Loudly.

November 3, 2011
Luke was so proud he made his own sandwich, "See mom, this is how you make it." (It had an inch of butter and dab of jelly.)

November 5, 2011
I tried my hardest to sleep this morning but it's about impossible when there is a butt in my face.

November 5, 2011
I've discovered that scrapbooking makes me swear a lot.

November 6, 2011
Landon to the twins, "You better listen to mom. You don't want her to be all crabby do you? Well, do you?"

November 6, 2011
Connor's Christmas list:
A real gun, a real whip, a real sword, a real dog.
no, no, no, NO!

November 7, 2011
Landon: "I had a dream that I saw a naked chicken and then I puked."

November 7, 2011
Luke: "Mom, I'm not hungry for supper. Can I have some candy corn?"

November 8, 2011
My new invention: children's car seats with optional strait jackets and muzzles.

A Mom's Life...in Status Updates

November 8, 2011
Here is proof that advertising works. I was tucking Landon in bed he said, "Mom, I need a TempurPedic mattress, it has foam, not springs."

November 9, 2011
I tried to introduce the boys to beets. You can imagine how well that turned out.

November 9, 2011
Driving home in the car Landon was whining:
Landon: "I'm thirsty."
Me: "Drink your saliva."
Landon: "And hungry."
Me: "Chew your saliva."

November 10, 2011
Evan's birthday summary: Buy cake, kids destroy cake, crying, timeouts, sing happy birthday, open presents, bury dog.

November 12, 2011
In the mail today we received: 1 whip and 3 light sabers. By bedtime we have 1 broken whip and 2 lightsabers.

November 13, 2011
The twins insist on climbing up on top of the van before getting in. Wouldn't it be easier to just to walk over and open the door?

November 13, 2011
So we were playing a little game at suppertime to see who could be the quietest the longest. And about 30 seconds into it Connor whispers out of the corner of his mouth "awkward."

November 14, 2011
Nothing gets the house cleaner quicker than having your lawyer come over to sign some papers. It's just too bad I missed the toothbrush under the table, the smushed grape on the wall and I would say the doorknob falling off was probably the highlight.

November 15, 2011
I just grabbed a couple sheets of toilet paper to blow my nose and it smelled like pee.

November 16, 2011
Bruce is trying to tell me I have PMS but the truth is that HE is just being REALLY annoying. What the heck is all this noise in the house? Seriously, who ate all the chocolate?

November 17, 2011
I asked the boys how school was Luke was so excited saying, "there was an army guy at our school for lunch and he drank THREE milks, 2 white and 1 chocolate!"

November 18, 2011
Connor: "God told me it's going to snow tomorrow."
Me: "What else did he tell you?"
Connor: "He told me poop comes from food."

November 18, 2011
I took the kids bowling and Landon said, "Geez, you must have to be 100 times richer than the richest person to own a bowling alley!"

November 19, 2011
Connor saw our wedding picture, pointed to the flower girls and asked, "Is this me and Luke when we were girls?"

November 20, 2011
Ponder this one. Connor, "How did Jesus make Santa if he was just a baby on Christmas?"

A Mom's Life...in Status Updates

November 20, 2011
I really think they should stop making white boys socks and just skip to the grayish color that they all end up being anyway!

November 21, 2011
Landon said he couldn't sleep because he kept thinking of skeletons coming to life. I told him to think of the skeletons dancing around all goofy (as I did a little dance). But he thought that was even scarier!

November 22, 2011
Apparently now I'm a "bad mom" because Landon's feet grew too big for his boots and supposedly in 3rd grade it's not "cool" to wear your mom's lady boots to school.

November 25, 2011
Decorating the house for Christmas is a 3 step process:
1. Decorate with the kids helping
2. Hide in the corner and drink to excess
3. Redecorate without the kids

November 27, 2011
At church this morning and there was a visiting priest and Connor whispered to me, "Why is there a different God here today?"

November 28, 2011
The twins started youth wrestling today. I figure since the ninja style didn't work out, we might as well try fighting WWE style!

November 29, 2011
I woke up to Luke saying, "Mom your breath smells like a rotten pumpkin."

December 3, 2011
Breakfast with Santa is not at all stressful.

December 4, 2011
Landon, "So I don't get it, how does this work. You get married and then in 9 months you go to the hospital and get a baby?"
Me: "BRUUUUUCE, Landon needs you."

December 7, 2011
Supernanny update...they are sending a psychologist out to our house to see if we are mentally stable for the show. Wonder if we will pass the test. It's questionable.

December 8, 2011
Landon: "Mom, my throat really hurts but I think it will feel better if I watch dancing skeletons on You Tube."

December 9, 2011
"Sometimes the toothfairy gets sick in the winter. I bet she will feel better tonight."

December 10, 2011
The boys are wrestling and Landon told the twins, "You guys can team up because I'm a one man warrior."

December 11, 2011
Connor: "I'm wondering, can the Supernanny fly like Superman?"

December 12, 2011
Landon: "Mom, why are you all 'nice talking' when you are on the phone but all 'yelling talking' when you are talking to us."

December 15, 2011
5 minutes until Supernanny knocks on the door. I already have my statement prepared, "It really isn't THAT bad, it's all in the editing."

A Mom's Life...in Status Updates

December 17, 2011
The Supernanny just got all up in my grill.
(Wow, I bet not too many people could say that.)

December 24, 2011
Santa didn't bring as many presents for Evan as he did his brothers. Probably because Evan doesn't know how to count yet.

December 26, 2011
I was telling Bruce that I was thinking about donating a kidney and he was like, "Oh no you don't! I might need that someday!"

December 28, 2011
Question of the day by Landon, "What's the deal, why is it called Facebook? Sometimes I see the whole body."

December 30, 2011
What you don't want to hear coming from a five year old, "Mom, quick do you have any duct tape?"

December 30, 2011
Landon: "Mom can you come and tuck me in? I need some love that will last 8 hours."

-2012-

Landon, 9; Luke & Connor, 6; Evan, 3

January 1, 2012
Bruce thinks it's a bad idea that I took the batteries out of the smoke alarm to put in a toy. But I think it's bad idea to listen to a whining kid for the rest of the evening.

January 2, 2012
I cannot tell a lie, I'm happy that the kids are going back to school tomorrow! Also, I ate dog food when I was 4 and stole a fridge magnet from a house party when I was in college. I told you I can't lie!

January 3, 2012
Connor is begging me to look on the computer to find a wishing well so he can wish for $2,000 to buy more wishing wells.

January 3, 2012
I had to remind the kids of the new house rules. You sit on the furniture. You do not pick it up and throw it!

January 4, 2012
A funny thing happened in my bed. Evan reached over to get the glass of water and spilled it all over Landon. Landon sat up and yelled at the top of his voice, "AWWWW! EVAN PEED ON MY HEAD."

January 4, 2012
So I put a big box of chocolates in Bruce's truck so I wouldn't be tempted to eat it. But now I want my box of chocolates back and Bruce is gone and I'm pissed at him for stealing my candy.

A Mom's Life...in Status Updates

January 4, 2012
The Supernanny people called to get an update on how things are going. I told them that I joined a Supernanny Support Group where we all wear crowns and call ourselves "beautiful princesses."

January 5, 2012
Lesson of the day: If you push the snooze alarm too many times, the kids will miss the school bus.

January 10, 2012
I explained to Landon that it's time for him to start to wear deodorant. He took a whiff and asked, "But why? It just smells like gym class."

January 11, 2012
Why is it that as soon as we see the bus coming up the driveway, one boy realizes he has to poop, one mysteriously loses a glove and then one decides he doesn't want to go to school anymore?

January 11, 2012
Quote of the day from Luke, "One time, when I was four I got a really tall wedgie."

January 12, 2012
Three people in Las Vegas asked me, "Are you from Minnesota?"
I do NOT have an accent. Everyone else talks weird.

January 15, 2012
I asked Landon what does he know about Martin Luther King Jr. and he said, "Well, I know he said the word "the."

January 19, 2012
You know you're getting old when the highlight of your day is putting on red snowflake flannel pajamas.

January 20, 2013
"The toothfairy is getting high tech and might have just sent the money right to your savings account. Let's call the bank and see."

January 21, 2012
Evan is re-organizing my rolodex.
What the heck, I still have a rolodex?

January 21, 2012
From TV Guide:
America's Supernanny Episode: "The Skluzacek Family"
Season 1, Episode 8
Episode Synopsis: Deborah helps a Minnesota couple with four unruly boys.

January 22, 2012
It's getting really annoying having to fight over the computer with a 3 year old. Seriously kid, go get your own computer!

January 22, 2012
Just went to my first youth wrestling tournament.
Correction: Just went to my LAST youth wrestling tournament.

January 22, 2012
Waiting for our Supernanny episode to air is like being pregnant. I want it to be over with but I don't want to go through all the pain to get there!

January 22, 2012
Landon came running downstairs complaining about sharing a room with Evan, "That's it! I'm done sleeping with that freak!"

January 23, 2012
I have an overwhelming urge to mix my two favorite foods together: Nutella and braunschweiger.

A Mom's Life...in Status Updates

January 24, 2012
Quote of day from Landon, "It's not fair, school wastes 5 days of fun!"

January 24, 2012
I have made great strides in my mothering abilities this year. My latest accomplishment was sewing up the holes in the boy's snowpants rather than duct taping them like I've done every other year.

January 27, 2012
The boys always complain about riding the bus every morning. So being a nice mom I drove them into school. But on the way Landon was sad saying, "I'm just thinking about how much fun I would be having on the bus right now."

January 28, 2012
Oops, I went upstairs to do the laundry but took a nap instead. I hate it when that happens.

January 31, 2012
Heading to Landon's spelling bee. Wonder if he can spell "incompetent mother" or "absentee father." (Just a little teaser of our Supernanny episode.)

February 2, 2012
I just came up with the BEST diet idea ever. You can eat whatever you want but you have to use chopsticks. 1 chopstick.

February 2, 2012
Blonde moment of the day: I went for a walk and was mad at myself because my ears were freezing and I should have worn a hat. Then 15 minutes later I realized my coat had a hood on it.

February 4, 2012
Random quote of the day by Landon, "I've decided that I like porcupines better in pictures then in real life."

February 5, 2012
You know a kid spends too much time on the computer when at church, during a prayer the priest pauses and Landon whispers to me, "Mom, I think he froze."

February 6, 2012
Walking down the sidewalk, Luke picks up a piece of sidewalk salt and eats it. When I told him not to eat it he asks, "But why? I eat it on the school bus all the time."

February 6, 2012
Question of the day by Landon, "Mom, what's a hippie freak?"

February 7, 2012
The boys won't eat tuna casserole but they love "Indiana Jones Noodles" which just happens to have the exact same ingredients.

February 8, 2012
I overheard Landon trying to sing this song, "Red paper cup, I FOLD you up."

February 8, 2012
While Bruce is recovering from surgery, Luke informed me that he will do all the dad stuff, like mow the grass, wear work gloves, drive the truck and do stuff with sharp knives.

February 9, 2012
I'm trying to explain to Bruce that pain pills and power tools are probably not a good combination.

A Mom's Life...in Status Updates

February 9, 2012
I just realized that maybe I do spoil Evan a little bit. He was knocking on the bathroom door and I asked who it was and he said, "It's Evan. Evan Cutie Bird."

February 11, 2012
I let the kids pick out a treat at the store. Landon picked a can of pop, Luke picked Skittles, Evan picked licorice and Connor picked BROCCOLI. (Whose child is this?)

February 12, 2012
Quote of the day: "Get that broccoli out of your ear! Now!"

February 12, 2012
Connor lost another tooth today. I better brush up on my "reasons the toothfairy didn't come." You know, just as a precaution.

February 13, 2012
In the tub, Luke opened his eyes underwater for the first time. I asked him if he saw anything under there and he said, "I saw Connor's fart!"

February 14, 2012
Luke's special prayer, "I pray for my family, water, food and bones."

February 15, 2012
Quote of the morning by Landon, "Our family would be less annoying if Evan went away."

February 16, 2012
I think I may regret this, but I just introduced the boys to "Talk to the hand!"

February 19, 2012
Landon's question of the day, "Mom, when can we get livestock?" Followed by, "Mom, what is livestock?"

February 21, 2012
I have a comedian for a son. Landon made up this joke tonight:
Q: What sounds like a snake and goes into the toilet?
A: Pisssssssssssssss

February 23, 2012
Seriously, with the use of only one arm Bruce can construct 4 handcrafted nightstands, but cannot load the dishwasher?

February 23, 2012
Landon's question of the day, "What's the big deal about head lice anyway?"

February 25, 2012
Landon: "Kids in Africa are lucky because they don't have to take swimming lessons."

February 26, 2012
Landon was wondering how he will know who he should marry. I told him that someday he will meet a nice woman, will fall in love and will want to spend the rest of your life with her. Landon thought a minute. "But does it have to be a woman?" Silence.
Landon: "Can it be a girl?"

February 28, 2012
How Connor eats a Subway sandwich:
1. remove all vegetables
2. dip sandwich in hot chocolate
3. enjoy

February 29, 2012
Connor stuck his head in my face and asked, "Mom, can you hear my ear buzzing?"

A Mom's Life...in Status Updates

March 1, 2012
So a random person called my cell phone and asked, "Is this the right number for the hair removal franchise?" Um, no, but tell me more.

March 1, 2012
Just remembering 6 years ago today when I gave birth twice. The first one all natural and the second one a C-section 20 minutes later. Double the fun!

March 2, 2012
Landon: "Are you born with a favorite color? Because I think I was."

March 2, 2012
Without a reasonable doubt I would easily be able to survive several months trapped in my vehicle consuming only the food scraps that I find on the floor.

March 2, 2012
Bruce and I have decided to blame all of our problems on growth spurts: Naughty kids...growth spurt
Cranky kids...growth spurt
Smelly kids...growth spurt
Messy house...growth spurt
Irritable mom...growth spurt
Annoying dad...growth spurt. (and on and on)

March 3, 2012
Today I learned that in a swimming suit emergency, 6 year old Connor can squeeze into size 18 month swimming trunks.

March 4, 2012
That poor piñata didn't stand a chance against the Skluzacek boys.

March 5, 2012
Landon: "I can't do my homework because Connor keeps putting crackers in his butt."

March 6, 2012
Landon and I are researching the state of Washington and he is INSISTING that George Washington was born there. It's going to be a long night.

March 6, 2012
Evan's outfit of choice today: a gun holster around his waist and a rosary around his neck, and nothing else.

March 7, 2012
Not my proudest moment, digging through the garbage looking for Landon's homework. I may have accidently thrown it away.

March 7, 2012
Connor: "Mom, I liked chicken when I lived in your belly but now I don't."

Mary 8, 2013
"Oh my, that silly toothfairy but the money in my pocket!"

March 9, 2012
Connor's lesson of the day, "If you are going to kiss, first you have to make your lips into raisins, like this." (as he puckers up)

March 11, 2012
I summed my day up in a poem:
Fly a kite...fly fly
Get it stuck in a tree...cry cry
Shoot it down with the gun...why why
Beer.

A Mom's Life...in Status Updates

March 12, 2012
Landon: "Can I have more ice cream?"
Me: "No!"
Landon: "That's bad parenting!"

March 13, 2012
Leave it to my dad to complain to the doctors at the hospital that he would "get better treatment at a large animal vet clinic."

March 14, 2012
Landon knew that the 50 stars on the U.S. flag are for the 50 states. I asked him what the red and white stripes represent. "Um, is it Dr. Suess's hat?"

March 16, 2012
Only a mother would be sewing on a monkey's tail at 2am.

March 17, 2012
You know it's St. Patrick's day when Luke finds a green colored potato chip and thinks for sure that a leprechaun put it in there!

March 20, 2012
Here are some of the chapter titles to my upcoming book...-
-The joys of bodily functions
-You put WHAT WHERE??
-And the mother of the year award goes to...
-When beer is the only option

March 21, 2012
Why is it that when I'm trying to do the dishes, someone starts licking my elbow?

March 23, 2012
I surprised the kids and rode the school bus home with them. I was pretty much the most popular girl on the bus, probably because I brought everyone candy.

March 25, 2012
I will always remember my 40th birthday as, "The day Bruce decided it was a good idea to buy each of the boys their own BB gun."

March 25, 2012
Birthday quote of the day by Landon: "You had a nice life when you were younger, maybe some good things will still happen to you now that you're old."

March 26, 2012
The twins got an invitation to a friend's birthday party and the first thing Luke asks, "Can I bring my new BB gun to the party??"

March 27, 2012
Why is it that I have a 3 year old computer genius, yet he still poops his pants?

March 27, 2012
Question of the day by Luke, "If I lose my head can I still keep my neck?"

March 28, 2012
Landon is already planning for the future. "Before I go to college I will have to get my own computer and my own Facebook."

March 29, 2012
Only in a houseful of boys would someone think of peeing in a squirt gun.

March 29, 2012
I just remembered the 2 reasons why I don't like coloring Easter eggs.
1. Kids
2. Eggs

A Mom's Life...in Status Updates

March 30, 2012
Connor: "I want to go baby hunting."
Translation: I want to shoot the BB gun.

April 2, 2012
Random thought of the day by Landon, "There are a lot of different ways you could fall in a lake."

April 4, 2012
I walk in the kitchen and spot Evan eating a stick of butter like a candybar. And I thought we were done eating condiments around here.

April 5, 2012
Our first campfire of the year ended with Connor crying, "I can't go to school anymore because I melted my shoe!"

April 5, 2012
Landon's question of the day, "How old do you have to be to be a teen?"

April 7, 2012
9 year old boy humor: "Mom, at recess I always hold onto my balls."

April 7, 2012
You know there is trouble when the Hershey's chocolate syrup bottle and Evan are missing.

April 7, 2012
Tucking Connor into bed, "Mom, don't forget to give my bag of slime a hug and kiss."

April 8, 2012
Whoever invented Easter basket grass should be introduced to an early grave.

April 9, 2012
On the radio they were talking about the Minnesota Twins and Luke was so excited, "Hey mom, Twins, they are talking about me and Connor!"

April 9, 2012
For some reason half of this family is afflicted with "gum stuck on my neck" disease!

April 10, 2012
Landon's words of wisdom for today, "Let me give you some advice. It's always Evan's fault."

April 10, 2012
At McDonalds, Landon says, "Mom, I think there's a spy here. See that guy in a fancy suit at McDonalds, that's suspicious!"

April 11, 2012
How many times a day do I have to say, "Put your pants on?"

April 14, 2012
Overheard the twins talking, "If you do that, you will have boogers in your poop!"

April 14, 2012
I was taking a shower and Landon yells upstairs, "Mom, someone's here. I think it's the Hobo Whippings" (He meant to say the Jehovah Witnesses.)

April 17, 2012
Landon was trying to explain The Flintstones to the twins, "You know that show, the guys with the feet."

April 19, 2012
Tried out my new Scentsy warmer tonight and discovered two Lego figures swimming in the melted wax.

A Mom's Life...in Status Updates

April 19, 2012
Dear Family, I cannot be held responsible for remembering where I hid your stuff. So stop bothering me with your "stuff" so I don't have to hide it in the first place. Love, mom

April 20, 2012
I learned that when you sign up for the "prepay" plan with the electric company you need to pay first and then get electricity second. Who knew?

April 21, 2012
Getting excited to run a 5k in a gorilla suit today. But Luke is worried because he thinks the cops are going to think we are real monkeys and shoot us.

April 22, 2012
Landon: "I think I should take a break from church, I get so tired of standing and listening."

April 23, 2012
I caught Connor going through the box of Honey Bunches of Oats and eating all of the honey nut clusters saying, "I love my honey balls."

April 24, 2012
How awesome is this, one boy is mowing the lawn, two are washing my car and one is looking for snakes. Well, 3/4 isn't bad.

April 25, 2012
Quote of the day, "NO RUNNING with the SNAKE JAR!!"

April 25, 2012
Landon informed me that everyday Connor buys a sucker from a girl on the bus. This may be why he has so many cavities and why my spare change is always missing.

April 29, 2012
Just spent the past 30 minutes trying to explain what "brunch" is to Landon. He doesn't quite get the concept. Remind me to never bring up "lupper."

May 1, 2012
Why did Evan give himself a haircut? "My hair was too big."

May 2, 2012
All the boys have light-up sandals. You know what that means. I'm a Walmart mom.

May 3, 2012
Landon sat in the front seat of the car and he noticed the blinker flashing and said, "Wow, that's weird, how does the car know which way you are going to turn?"

May 3, 2012
Luke's letter to the tooth-fairy, "Bring me lots of money so I can buy 100 dogs."

May 5, 2012
Luke was looking all sad and I asked him what's wrong. "Why did you name me Luke? I want my name to be Indiana Jones."

May 7, 2012
Luke: "I don't like Grandma."
Me: "Why would you say that?"
Luke: "Because she calls hotdogs wieners."

May 8, 2012
It's pouring rain so I run like heck to get to my car, only to end up standing there like a dummy, digging in my purse for my keys.

A Mom's Life...in Status Updates

May 9, 2012
Luke: "Mom, Connor is hitting me with his bag of money!"
Me: "Bag of money? Where?"

May 10, 2012
Landon informed me that if he was a millionaire, he wouldn't spend any money. Because if he did, then he wouldn't have a million dollars anymore.

May 11, 2012
There is nothing quite as disgusting as going to wash my face and the washcloth smells like Bruce's underarm.

May 11, 2012
I've inherited the, "I'm going to throw that dang toy out the window!" saying from my dad. But the difference is that he would actually throw it out. And now, I strangely admire him for that.

May 12, 2012
Quote of the day, "BRUCE...where did you hide my good hoe?"

May 13, 2012
My perfect mother's day gift: to have a few hours away from those who call me mother.

May 13, 2013
Our microwave died. So there will be no popcorn for movie night. Which means no popcorn all over the couches and carpet, so I'm ok with it. Until tomorrow, then we will all starve.

May 13, 2012
Luke's note to the toothfairy, "Give me a billion dollars so I can buy a microwave."

May 14, 2012
Luke was actually disappointed that the tooth-fairy didn't leave him 1 billion dollars. He glared at his $1.50 and gave it to me. Hello beer fund.

May 14, 2012
How is it that a tiny wrinkle in my sock drives me crazy, yet the kids can walk around with half the sandbox in their shoes!

May 15, 2012
Connor's question of the day: "Do you have to pay to be a Skluzacek?"

May 16, 2012
Tonight Evan stuck his fluoride tablet up his nose. I finally got it out with a tweezers... and he still wanted to eat it!

May 17, 2012
Quote of the day by Evan, "When I grow up I want to be a zombie so I can die people."

May 19, 2012
Here's an excerpt from Landon's paper on oral hygiene. "I think you should brush twice a day because then your teeth don't fall out and you look good for school pictures."

May 20, 2012
Overheard coming from the bathtub, "Butts Ahoy!"

May 20, 2012
2 years of honeymoon,
8 years of blur,
2 years of "what have we done"
=12 years of married bliss. Happy Anniversary Bruce.

A Mom's Life...in Status Updates

May 22, 2012
The next time Luke suggests that we bring a band-aid with on our bike ride, I need to listen and just grab the whole box.

May 23, 2012
Wondering if the kids' last day of kindergarten and 3rd grade will result in mom's first day of Prozac.

May 24, 2012
Question of the day by Connor, "How does God see us when it's cloudy?"

May 25, 2012
Landon: "Why is Obama always raising taxes?"
Me: "Do you even know what taxes are??"
Landon: "Electricity."

May 26, 2012
Landon: "Geez, if I had a time portal I would be rich by now."

May 27, 2012
Luke: "Mom, your breath smells like old fashioned teeth."

May 27, 2012
I love hay wagon rides. It's like riding in a limo, except you get straw stuck in your butt.

May 28, 2012
Quote of the day by Luke, "Mom, when I was a baby you looked weird but when I grew up you looked beautiful."

May 29, 2012
You can tell it's been a long, hard day when I get home from work and Grandma has all the boys praying the rosary.

May 30, 2012
Connor is sick this morning and said, "I hate puking in the summer, it wastes all my fun."

May 30, 2012
It's been one of those days. I was lying on the kitchen floor trying to fish a bouncy ball from under the stove and then I just decide to stay there. It was a nice quiet 10 minutes, until they found me.

May 30, 2013
Connor was all sad and asked, "When I go to college will they know I had to go to the principal's office three times?"

May 31, 2012
I was making supper and Landon had the nerve to ask me for an appetizer! What does he think this is Applebee's?

June 1, 2012
The nice thing about camping in our backyard is that I can sneak back into the house and crawl into bed.

June 3, 2012
Landon: "The only fun part of church is communion because I'm usually starving by then."

June 5, 2012
When a Walmart mom goes to Target, "Excuse me sir, where are your nuts located?"

June 6, 2012
Me: "Ok everyone, can we PLEASE not talk about poop at the supper table for once?"
The boys: "Ok."
Landon to Luke: "You have dirty underwear."

A Mom's Life...in Status Updates

June 7, 2012
Driving to school Landon says, "You're the best mom I could ever ask for. Can I steer the car?"

June 8, 2012
Heading out to the pool and Luke said, "Mom, that's a nice dress." That would be my swimming suit.

June 11, 2012
We had a great family party until the electricity went out and Connor started yelling, "We're all gonna die!"

June 11, 2012
The boys can't seem to take a walk without describing everything they see: "That house is messy. That dog is pooping. That lady is old. That guy's pants are falling down."

June 13, 2012
I made the mistake of letting Landon hold the GPS in the car. "Mom, you're going 1 mile over the speed limit. Now you're going 10 miles over the speed limit. MOM!"

June 13, 2012
Have you ever forgotten about a load of clothes in the washer for a couple of days but still put them in the dryer, with a few extra dryer sheets and then just hope for the best?

June 14, 2012
Two very heated topics of discussion at our house tonight:
1. Does Life cereal make you dead?
2. Can seahorses go to jail?

June 16, 2012
Somehow I managed to sleep until 9am. No one sat on my head, pulled off my blankets or yelled in my ear. And the kids didn't bother me either!

June 17, 2012
Evan was naming colors of the crayons, "Red, orange, blue, chocolate milk."

June 18, 2012
I was telling Bruce that pretty soon Connor was going to be blonde from the sun and Connor yelled, "WHAT? I DON'T WANT TO BE BLIND!"

June 20, 2012
I was not feeling well so I was lying on the couch. Evan thought he would be nice and brought over a dirty potholder for a pillow and a damp towel for a blanket.

June 22, 2012
I think Wii games should qualify as a tax deduction under the 'mental health' section. They are totally saving my sanity today.

June 22, 2012
I really wish pharmacies would deliver meds when you are sick. I have an idea, the liquor store delivers beer and I'll ask them to pick up my prescription on way. Think it will work?

June 22, 2012
Only in small towns will the liquor store stop and pick up your prescription at the pharmacy on their way to deliver your beer.

June 23, 2012
Evan just informed me that he wants a baby and a dog. No and No.

June 23, 2012
I told the kids that we are going to be "unplugged" this week. And when I say we, I mean them.

A Mom's Life...in Status Updates

June 23, 2012
Today Evan asked grandma, "Are you a boy or a girl?"

June 24, 2012
Coming from the other room, I hear Evan yelling, "MOM, my boogers are falling down!"

June 25, 2012
Evan just informed me, "I want to buy a new girlfriend for my house."

June 27, 2012
We experimented with making frozen waffles on the grill. I wouldn't recommend it.

June 29, 2012
Connor dropped his Nintendo DS in the toilet. I guess he was multi-tasking.

June 29, 2012
Landon, "Can you and dad go to Peru so I can stay overnight at our cousin's house?"

July 1, 2012
Out of the blue Landon asks, "Mom, when you die can I have your Kindle?"

July 2, 2012
Luke's financial advice, "Dad wastes all his money on the house and his truck. He should buy us tons and tons of video games!"

July 4, 2012
Connor: "I really want to go to the bank so I can see all the treasure chests full of money."

July 5, 2012
"I bet the toothfairy didn't come because she was scared of all the fireworks last night."

July 5, 2012
Our main conversation at supper tonight was Monkey brains. Thank you again Indiana Jones.

July 7, 2012
I should start a campaign to ban pockets in all kids clothes! They just fill them with nonessential things like sand, marshmallows, crayons and bugs.

July 7, 2012
Poor Evan has diarrhea and questioned me, "Mom, when are you going to fix my butt?"

July 8, 2012
In a matter of one day Evan was potty trained, the twins learned how to swim and Landon sprouted hairy legs.

July 9, 2012
I was singing "Wheels on the Bus" in the car and Evan kept yelling from the back seat, "Turn it Down!"

July 10, 2012
Question of the day by Landon, "Why are some boobs all flobby?" followed by hand gestures down to the belly button.

July 11, 2012
It's just wrong when a 3 year old, in Spongebob underwear, dances around and sings, "I'm sexy and I know it."

July 12, 2012
Luke, "Mom, you're not fat, you just have extra skin."

July 12, 2012
I have the whole house to myself I'm going to do something wild and crazy. Something that I can only do when I'm alone. Light a candle.

A Mom's Life...in Status Updates

July 16, 2012
I hate it when I forget to tell Bruce important stuff, like we're refinancing the house.

July 16, 2012
Connor, "Mom, you should lay another egg and have a girl this time."

July 17, 2012
Supper discussion, Does Indiana Jones like grilled cheese? The consensus was "He has to like it because he's American."

July 18, 2012
When you hear someone yelling "blood" from inside a bounce house it's pretty much guaranteed that it's one of my boys.

July 19, 2012
How is it that kids can make a perfectly crappy day, even crappier?

July 20, 2012
Landon: "Mom, can I cut up all your old dishtowels?"

July 22, 2012
It's been one of those days in the Skluzacek house when I had to turn on the garbage disposal just for some peace and quiet!

July 23, 2012
"Mom, can we PLEASE play on the computer? Then we won't annoy you." Now that's a compelling argument.

July 24, 2012
Quote of the day by Landon, "Sometimes when I sneeze 3 or 4 times, I get dizzy and fall down."

July 25, 2012
I was just trying to make small talk with a guy in line at the store:
Me: "So where are you from?"
Guy: "My mother's womb."
(awkward silence)

July 28, 2012
School supplies are all purchased. Now we just need school, only 45 more days.

July 29, 2012
Highlight of our evening, Landon pulling a piece of popcorn out of his belly button.

July 30, 2012
Luke was upset about the seeds in his watermelon, "MOM, there are peanuts in my watermelon!"

July 31, 2012
I've learned with 4 boys in the house it is not wise to have a magazine rack next to the toilet, unless you like to read "Peeople" Magazine.

August 2, 2012
Landon: "What did you and dad do on your first date?"
Me: "We went to a movie."
Landon: "Was it The Lion King?"

August 3, 2012
We were watching them interview an Olympic gold medal winner and Connor looked concerned and said, "I don't know what I will say when I win."

August 3, 2012
Me: "Quit fighting! Would Jesus hit his brother?"
Boys: "He didn't have a brother!"

A Mom's Life...in Status Updates

August 5, 2012
The best thing about weddings...free beer.
The worst thing about weddings...free beer.

August 5, 2012
Dear son, I'm sorry your balloon broke, but seriously you just got it 5 minutes ago...get over it!

August 6, 2012
Evan's favorite saying is, "I love you all the time," except for when it's, "I hate you all the time."

August 7, 2012
Connor was checking himself out in the mirror, "I really like my face. It's cute."

August 9, 2012
Me to the boys: "You cannot marry your mom, your sister or your aunt."
Boys: "That's not fair!!"

August 9, 2012
Watching the Olympic divers and I mentioned that one had too big of a splash and Landon said, "Well, just think about the big splash you would make."

August 10, 2012
Landon: "Do you like doing laundry?"
Me: "No"
Landon: "I can tell."
Me: "How?"
Landon: "I don't have any clean shorts."

August 11, 2012
Saturday mornings we power clean the house and Evan informed me, "You clean like a boy."

August 11, 2012
I told the boys that they have to get shoes with laces because they need to learn how to tie their shoes. Landon, "No, I want Velcro; it's a sacrifice I'm willing to make."

August 12, 2012
Connor: "Mom, I colored a picture for you. That will be $3.00."

August 13, 2012
Luke had his tonsils out today and Connor was concerned, "When will Luke be better so we can fight again?"

August 15, 2012
Wow, I totally forgot I had a garden.

August 15, 2012
I was discussing the George Clooney vs. Brad Pitt debate and declared, "I like George!" Landon overheard and said, "But, I thought you liked dad."

August 17, 2012
Only in a house full of boys do you get a goodnight fart along with every goodnight hug.

August 18, 2012
I told the boys to wipe their face before we get in the car and Connor whispered to Luke, "We must be going somewhere really fancy."

August 18, 2012
When your 3-year-old starts yelling, "Mom, DON'T come here!" You should probably go there.

August 20, 2012
Landon is a tough guy, "I will knock you down like a piece of cucumber off the table."

A Mom's Life...in Status Updates

August 21, 2012
Landon's odd question of the day, "Mom, can you get me some Borax?"

August 22, 2012
A big thanks to Auntie Laura for teaching the boys the fine art of armpit farting. I'm sure this is a skill that will bring them far in life.

August 23, 2012
Landon, "Mom, what's a period?"
Me, "Um, what do you mean?" (deep breath)
Landon, "You know, like 5th period."

August 23, 2012
So I made the huge mistake of asking the boys what they wanted for supper.
Connor: "I'll take some poop"
Landon: "What kind?"
Connor: "Big and brown"
Landon: "We are out of stock."
Luke: "How about diarrhea?"
Landon: "Ok, do you want pee with that?"

August 24, 2012
Non-farm boy Landon was explaining to the twins, "You can easily milk a cow by pulling on their gutters."

August 25, 2012
Luke and Connor were with Bruce and Evan keeps asking when "his twins" are coming home.

August 26, 2012
Sometimes all it takes to make the kids behave is the promise of seeing a dead mole on the driveway.

August 27, 2012
Random: I had a dream I was in the high school marching band and I played the slinky.

August 26, 2012
On our evening walk the boys were listing ways that you could die:
-fall off a cliff
-fall in hot lava
-get bitten by a snake
-get eaten by a bear
-fall on a fork

August 27, 2012
Landon's math brain at work again, "I figured something out, every 3 years you have a kid or two. It's time for another one."

August 28, 2012
It scared me when I went out to throw the trash bag in the garage and the cat ran right in front of me. Then realized we don't have a cat.

August 29, 2012
At Chuck E Cheese, the "prize" lady gave each of the boys a free plastic whistle for the ride home. She is the devil.

August 31, 2012
The nice thing about bringing the boys over to visit Grandma Skluzacek is that after we leave I know we will be getting A LOT of extra prayers!

August 31, 2012
Tucking Evan into bed he informed me, "Nemo is not a zombie."

September 1, 2012
In the vehicle after leaving a breakfast buffet, I notice the twins sitting in the backseat with fists full of bacon.

September 1, 2012
Evan: "Can I have a peanut butter and purple sandwich."

A Mom's Life...in Status Updates

September 2, 2012
Mysteriously all of the boy's toothbrushes were missing, until Luke pulled them out from under the bathroom rug where he was "keeping them safe."

September 4, 2012
I informed the boys that their new bus driver's name is Milt and Connor said, "I think I will just call him John."

September 6, 2012
Deep thoughts by Connor, "I figured out how to get to heaven... when you turn 99 you have to start being good."

September 7, 2012
Landon: "Mom, are you supposed to put the butter on the bread before or after you put it in the toaster?"
Me: "After"
Landon: "Oops"

September 9, 2012
I was telling Landon that he would have his golden birthday when he turns 13. He thought about it for a minute and said, "Wait a minute, so does that mean that I already missed my bronze and silver birthdays?"

September 10, 2012
Landon's question of the day, "IS Santa real? I must know before I die!"

September 12, 2012
Hey kids, I just ordered Netflix. See you in a month when the free trial expires.

September 14, 2012
Landon's alarm clock was going off and he yelled, "Hurry Evan and press the space bar." (When I was a kid we called it the snooze button.)

September 15, 2012
Sparklers + Skluzacek boys = Kung Fu Sparklers

September 16, 2012
Zoo: A place where the kids like to try to climb walls, collect plastic figurines and occasionally look at the animals.

September 16, 2012
At the zoo I told Evan to look at the monkey. He said, "No mom, that's an Orangutan."

September 17, 2012
We saw a skunk run into the woods and Landon was disappointed because he wanted to see the, "green cloud of stinkyness."

September 20, 2012
Landon: "I think SPAM stands for "Super Porky Animated Meat."

September 20, 2012
Bought a $1 back scratcher at Target today to replace my $1 husband who won't scratch my back because his "hands are tired."

September 21, 2012
There was a Santa suit in a plastic bag in the basement and Connor looked in horror, "Why would Santa throw his suit away?"

September 23, 2012
The boys won 7 cakes at the church festival cake walk. That's a cake for every day this week. Sweet.

September 24, 2012
I was all excited to tell Bruce that I won a quilt and all he had to say was, "I hope it doesn't have a lot of squares."

A Mom's Life...in Status Updates

September 24, 2012
Landon: "Mom, what does it feel like to get electrocuted?"
Me: "Why?"
Landon: "Because I think I just was."

September 26, 2012
Happiness is finding a stray M&M in the bottom of your purse! Sadness is realizing it's a Skittles.

September 27, 2012
Me to the boys: "Do you really think I like yelling at you guys day after day?"
Landon: "No, but you're so good at it."

September 28, 2012
Connor is working hard on his reading because he "wants to go to college for free." Guess who slipped into the #1 spot?

September 30, 2012
Connor: "You are the best mom and the best Chris."

October 1, 2012
I miss the old days when math books had the odd numbers answers in the back of the book. They don't do that anymore. I checked. 4th grade math is hard.

October 4, 2012
Landon: "I was wondering, do I have a step-mom?"

October 5, 2012
Some people have guard dogs. We have a guard possum. The problem is that it's guarding the garage from us. And it's dirty, smelly, messy and poops everywhere. I guess it fits right in.

October 6, 2012
It's a "Go watch Netflix" kind of day.

October 6, 2012
Luke: "Landon punched me."
Landon: "No I didn't, I was just feeling his cheek with my knuckle."

October 8, 2012
I was driving and was grumbling about taking a wrong turn and Connor said, "Mom, are we lost? I should have brought my globe with!"

October 9, 2012
Only in a houseful of boys are grilled cheese sandwiches fashioned into guns and the tomato soup is the carnage.

October 10, 2012
Me: "Ok boys, any swearing and you will get your mouth washed out with soap!"
Connor: "That's just wasting soap."

October 12, 2012
Evan counting: "One, two...ten, eleventeen."

October 15, 2012
Our electricity went out and Evan yelled, "Mom, the TV needs new batteries!"

October 18, 2012
Cleaning out my medicine cupboard and found 2 bottles of Holy Water. You never know when I will need that as a last resort.

October 18, 2012
The joys of motherhood:
Landon: "Mom, I feel like I'm going to puke."
Me: "Here's a bucket just in case."
Landon: "Oops, I just puked on the carpet."

A Mom's Life...in Status Updates

October 20, 2012
Is it just me or is coming home early before the kids are in bed just a waste of a night out?

October 21, 2012
Lesson of the day: A boxelder bug can survive being cooked in the microwave for 2 minutes.

October 21, 2012
I am super excited for the day when everyone can scrape out their own pumpkin guts.

October 24, 2012
Question of the day: "Mom, have you ever met a Mary that you don't like?

October 25, 2012
Luke snuck away from the table and Connor slid over onto his chair. When Luke came back he whispered to Connor, "Thanks for being me."

October 27, 2012
Today's adventure: the boys booby-trapped their rooms with dental floss all the dental floss in the house.

October 27, 2012
I told Luke not to bother writing down a $380 Lego set on his Christmas list. But Connor told him, "Write it down anyway because Santa has lots of money!"

October 28, 2012
I figured something out, I will only feel old when I'm older then the US President. Therefore I will always vote for the old guy.

October 29, 2012
I hid the Halloween candy so good that I can't even find it!

October 29, 2012
You know it's going to be a bad day when the school bus driver has to call the house to wake everyone up.

October 31, 2012
Halloween. It's the one day of the year where it's socially acceptable to wear my Little House on Prairie dress and bonnet.

October 31, 2012
When we were trick-or-treating, Connor was so excited about all the candy he said, "I hope this is real and not a dream!"

October 31, 2012
When we got home from trick-or-treating Connor poured out all of his candy and told Luke, "This is a miracle!"

November 1, 2012
In the reject pile this morning: pretzels and Almond Joy.

November 1, 2012
Landon: "What kind of candy is this?"
Me: "Sixlets"
Landon: "That's dumb, there's more than six."

November 2, 2012
The twins were fighting and I yelled, "What is going on here?"
Connor, "It's not us, the candy started it!"

November 3, 2012
Luke's question of the day, "How do you speak horse?"

November 3, 2012
I was telling the boys that many years ago I ran 26 miles in a marathon and all they had to say was, "So did you win?"

A Mom's Life...in Status Updates

November 5, 2012
6 year olds rationale for who they would vote for:
Connor: "Obama because he's getting older."
Luke: "Romney because he hasn't had a turn yet."

November 7, 2012
Another example of what you do not want to hear coming from the bathroom...
Me: "Evan, what's taking so long in the bathroom?"
Evan: "I'm putting my lips on."

November 9, 2012
This morning a huge fight broke out over who gets the sugar crumbs from the bottom of the cereal bag. Luckily, I have the longest arms and won.

November 11, 2012
Dear family member,
When there is a loud explosion followed by a moaning noise coming from the bathroom, you don't have to yell across the house, "I have diarrhea." We already know.

November 11, 2012
Connor: "I really want a wishbone. Mom, can you go kill a chicken?"

November 13, 2012
Me: "Why must you whine about everything?"
Landon: "Why must you whine about me whining about everything?"

November 14, 2012
Whenever I hear the phrase "muffin top" it totally makes me hungry for a gigantic, lemon poppyseed muffin.

November 15, 2012
There's a pattern when the boys watch cartoons: 15 minutes of quiet, 5 minutes of fighting. Darn commercials.

November 16, 2012
I was home all day cleaning and obviously failed to look in the mirror because when the boys came home from school the first thing they said was, "Mom, what happened to your face?"

November 18, 2012
Quote of the day by Landon, "If I were the only kid in this family I wouldn't be so crabby."

November 18, 2012
Since "Grandma Moo-Moo" is no longer living on the farm with cows, she will now be referred to as "Grandma Townhome."

November 20, 2012
Landon sulking over his homework, "I wish I could go back in time and tell them not to invent cursive."

November 20, 2012
For some reason I really want a grandfather clock. But I refuse to get a used one because I'm afraid it will be haunted.

November 21, 2012
I was explaining to Bruce that people should hug for at least 6 seconds to get the optimum mood enhancing benefits. He shuddered and ran into the garage.

November 23, 2012
Yesterday, when I was in the ER with Luke, the nurse asked if he was allergic to anything. He whispered in a sick voice, "I'm allergic to unicorns."

November 24, 2012
Notice: The Skluzacek Ranch for Wayward Boys will temporarily be renamed the Influenza Inn.

A Mom's Life...in Status Updates

November 25, 2012
I asked Bruce and the non-sick kids to kindly take the long way home after church. Via Mexico.

November 26, 2012
Quote of the day by Luke, "Mom, remember when I was 4 and I was sick and you gave me a blanket. That was nice."

November 26, 2012
"Elfie" (Elf on the Shelf) showed up tonight. The boys were good for the first few minutes but then started fighting over who Elfie liked best.

November 27, 2012
Quote of the day by Luke, "Elfie needs glasses so he can see how naughty Connor is being."

November 28, 2012
Another meal gets a bad review from my critics.
Luke: "Mom this supper tastes like criminal food."

November 28, 2012
I asked Landon if he could name the continents. He could name three: North America, South America and Arizona.

November 29, 2012
Why is it that, the boys lose the $10 mittens in one day, but the $1 cheapo ones stick around all season?

November 29, 2012
Luke: "Mom, Connor spit on my head."
Connor: "No I didn't. I was drooling."

November 30, 2012
This morning I stared at the cup of toothbrushes and had no idea which one was mine. This is why we should never get new toothbrushes.

December 1, 2012
The first time (and only time) I wear my new hat Connor says, "Mom, I like your hat, you look like a servant."

December 1, 2012
Connor's Christmas List: "I want everything except girl stuff."

December 2, 2012
Landon: "I am so angry. Luke drew a picture of me with glasses, a heart on my shirt and a top-hat. How rude."

December 2, 2012
Teaching lesson of the day:
Me: "Boys don't EVER do drugs."
Boys: "What are drugs?"
Me: "They are bad, illegal things...like marijuana and meth."
Landon: "What? Math is illegal??'

December 3, 2012
Connor spotted some of his old papers and artwork in the garbage. It must have "fallen" in there.

December 3, 2012
Landon's thought of the day, "I know why people look younger when they go to heaven, because if they didn't, it would just be a giant nursing home."

December 4, 2012
Me: "Evan, aren't you hungry, you didn't eat any supper."
Evan: "I'm not hungry for yucky food."

December 4, 2012
Landon: "Is it true that girls like bad boys who ride motorcycles and wear bandannas on their head?"
Me: "No, girls like boys who are smart and who can clip their own fingernails."

A Mom's Life...in Status Updates

December 5, 2012
Connor has his wedding day all planned out:
"When I get married I'm going to jump into a mud puddle, give my wife all the mud and then run away naked."

December 5, 2012
Luke was too scared to go to bed so I told him that his guardian angel will protect him. But Luke responded, "Mom, don't you know that guardian angels aren't real. They are made in China."

December 6, 2012
We took the boys out to eat and discovered the perfect, stress-free way to dine in style. The boys sit in a booth and Bruce and I sit at a table, on the other side of the restaurant.

December 7, 2012
An excerpt from Landon's paper on 'How to survive school:'
"Listen to your teacher and don't just look around the room all day."

December 8, 2012
Ok kids, if I'm going to help you get on your snow pants, boots, coat, mittens, scarf, hat, then you need to actually go out in the snow. Not just stand in the garage and say it's too cold!

December 9, 2012
Went to grandma's house after it snowed and Luke said, "Look mom, grandma painted her roof white."

December 9, 2012
Bruce: "Boys, everyone remember this day as "The day we played UNO" because it's never going to happen again."

December 10, 2012
Have you ever looked at your child and thought, "WHO ARE YOU?"

December 9, 2012
Connor: "I really want something for Christmas."
Mom: "What?"
Connor: "You know, it starts with a P."
Mom: "A P? I'm not sure, what is it?"
Connor: "What I've always wanted, a puter!"

December 12, 2012
The twins were washing the dishes and next thing you know they are standing naked in the kitchen with dishtowels taped to their body.

December 13, 2012
Luke: "Geez, dad is so strict about losing air. If we leave the door open he yells at us to shut it."

December 16, 2012
The boys all got remote control cars. It was tons of fun until they realized that one remote could control all of them. Then it was just fun for one.

December 17, 2012
Family monopoly night, it turns out that I am a jailbird top hat and Evan is a bank robbing thimble.

December 17, 2012
Luke's nighttime problems:
"Connor licked my pillow."
"Connor is smelling my blanket."
"Connor picked his nose and wiped it on my cheek."

December 18, 2012
I get confused every time, Evan calls orange juice "apple apple juice" and apple juice is called "orange juice." I've learned to just offer him milk. Less drama.

A Mom's Life...in Status Updates

December 21, 2012
While I was getting my nails done at the salon, a guy rushed in and asked for a gift certificate. But he asked for them to make the date 11/21 instead of 12/21 so it looks like he planned ahead. Smart man.

December 22, 2012
Wrapping gifts, I didn't like that most of the boys presents were so small (expensive, but small) so I wrapped everything in the biggest boxes I could find. In this case size does matter.

December 23, 2012
At our family Christmas, the adults tried to be super sneaky by hiding the tray of Christmas cookies from the kids in the microwave. It was all good until Connor turned on the microwave.

December 24, 2012
Bruce will soon be bringing home the boy's Christmas present. A real, live DOG! Lord help us.

December 24, 2012
The boys were playing with the dog and Connor said, "This is the best Christmas ever! If this is only a dream, I will cry in my bed."

December 24, 2012
Ahh, the smells of Christmas: fireplace, cookies, dog poop.

December 24, 2012
You know I'm overly exhausted when I actually just thought to myself, maybe I shouldn't set the security system in case Santa needs to use the door.

December 26, 2012
Evan has pink eye and he thinks he got it because, "Connor farted in my eye."

December 26, 2012
Have you ever put all your bills in the bill box and then forget that you have a bill box?

December 27, 2012
Watching the boys, I can honestly say that I've never had the urge to throw myself on the ground and slide across the floor.

December 28, 2012
Evan was shooing the dog out of his room saying "I need alone time." And it begins.

December 28, 2012
Dear family,
I spent all day washing your bedding, including your nasty pillow pets. Please refrain from drooling and other bodily functions.
Love, Mom

December 29, 2012
At breakfast Evan randomly informed us, "I like dynamite and eating candy."

A Mom's Life...in Status Updates

-2013-

Landon, 10; Luke & Connor, 7; Evan, 4

January 1, 2013
It's official, the dog has become the favorite child. She is the only one in this house who actually listens to me, she keeps the kitchen floor spotless and she cleans up her own vomit.

January 2, 2013
Question of the day by Landon, "Dad, are you at the age when you stop growing and start shrinking?"

January 3, 2013
Dear children, if you wake up in the middle of the night and have to go pee, don't cry and wander around like a zombie, just go to the bathroom.

January 3, 2013
After giving Bruce a hug goodnight, Luke informed him, "Dad, you better shave because your bristles are getting pokey."

January 4, 2013
Evan was telling me that he loves our house and wants to live here forever. Thought to self, well in your case forever is 14 more years. Enjoy.

January 5, 2013
Why must Bruce always try to dampen my shopping experience by asking me to stop at Menards.

January 6, 2013
It's a good day when I take a nap and the house is still standing when I get up.

January 7, 2013
When I was a youngster my dad warned me to look out for pig eyelashes in hotdogs. Now my boys search for pig eyelashes. I love family traditions.

January 8, 2013
It's a rough morning around here when Landon whines, "Why does that dumb alarm clock have to destroy my sleep?"

January 9, 2013
I successfully smuggled out 4 pickled squid from the China buffet to show the kids. But unfortunately my "supper surprise" didn't go over too well.

January 10, 2013
I drove a different route to Grandma's house and Evan yelled from the backseat, "Mom, you're on the wrong racetrack!"

January 11, 2013
It's mommy and Evan day, otherwise known as "mom cleans the house and Evan plays on the computer day."

January 12, 2013
Not only is Luke allergic to "unicorns" he also informed me that he is allergic to "twins."

January 13, 2013
The first words out of Landon's mouth on his birthday morning, "I'M A DECADE TODAY!!"

January 13, 2013
Bruce to Luke: "Why are you so cute?"
Luke: "Cuz you and mom made me cute."
Connor (yelling from the other room): "Mom, you made me a pain in the butt."

January 15, 2013
Trying to get the kids upstairs to bed, "Come on people, let's go!" Connor, "Where are we going? South America?"

A Mom's Life...in Status Updates

January 16, 2013
Coming from Landon's bedroom: "Mom, quick get a towel, I just spilled my invisible ink!"

January 16, 2013
Connor wanted me to fix his closet door, so I pointed to Bruce and told him to ask the maintenance man. Bruce's response, "That guy was fired."

January 16, 2013
Tonight, I accidentally rang the doorbell and the twins jumped out of bed to see if there's a robber at the door. Yes, the robbers always ring before entering.

January 18, 2013
Experienced that awkward moment when you get to the entrance of Walmart and the automatic doors don't open and then you stand there like an idiot trying to figure out how to get in.

January 19, 2013
I find it hard to take a 10-year-old boy in tightie whities seriously.

January 19, 2013
I put on fake eyelashes and when I showed the family, Connor thought I had "angry eyes."

January 21, 2013
Conversation between twins:
Connor: "I have to go poop."
Luke: "Good luck."

January 23, 2013
Luke told Bruce he wants a "man hug" instead of a "baby hug." It appears that a man hug is a regular hug with 2 pats on the back.

January 24, 2013
Dear Luke: if you want a drink of water, go get a cup. Don't suck the water out of an old washcloth.

January 24, 2013
Connor has two requirements for his future bride. "I want to marry someone who is pretty and knows how to read."

January 25, 2013
Bruce is trying to convince me that he should buy a skid loader. I'm trying to convince him that I should buy a Coach purse. My argument is a lady NEEDS a purse; a man doesn't NEED a skid loader.

January 26, 2013
Connor was looking through my jewelry box and was so surprised, "Mom, you have 4 rings! I didn't know you were married four times?"

January 26, 2013
Tonight the boys watched figure skating with me, probably because I didn't tell them about Ultimate Fighting Championship on the other channel.

January 27, 2013
Connor: "Mom, is anything impossible?"
Me: "Anything is possible if you put your mind to it."
Connor: "Good cuz I want to fart all the way to the moon."

January 27, 2013
Luke was asking for fake wine with supper and I said, "No, it's only for special occasions." Then he asked, "Well, isn't every day special?" We had fake wine.

January 28, 2013
Every time the school has "pajama day" I have a tiny anxiety attack worrying that it's the wrong day.

January 29, 2013
Bruce is annoyed with me for not knowing the density and strength of a cow's horn.

A Mom's Life...in Status Updates

January 30, 2013
Landon: "Mom, if I had a trillion dollars I would make you a princess. It might cost a million but it really wouldn't hurt my budget."

January 31, 2013
Conversation while Luke was getting his haircut.
Hair stylist: "So...do you have a girlfriend?"
Luke: "No! And I'm done talking to you."

February 1, 2013
For family movie night we watched our Supernanny episode. Connor covered his eyes and said "This is so painful!!"

February 2, 2013
I was putting on makeup and Connor asked, "What's that?"
Me: "Mascara"
Connor: "Ma-scara? Why do you want to scare people?"

February 2, 2013
Working on taxes and trying to figure out a way to deduct BB guns and tooth fairy expenses.

February 3, 2013
Bruce's idea of supper for the boys: pears and jalapeno poppers.

February 3, 2013
Landon: "Mom, Dad stenched up my blankets with his farts."

February 3, 2013
The questions I got from Landon during church had nothing at all to do with church:
"Is gum biodegradable?"
"How many volcanoes are there in the world?"
"What is middle school REALLY like?"

February 4, 2013
Landon: "Luke ate some of my brownie, so I put glue all over his shirt. Now we're even."

February 5, 2013
Some days I just want to say to everyone I meet, "Don't judge me because I have dried up boogers smeared across my shirt. I have four boys."

February 9, 2013
At Culver's a policeman had someone pulled over on the road in front of our window and Landon said, "I bet he's just picking up his supper."

February 10, 2013
Our family monopoly game was ruined when someone put a booger on someone else's thimble.

February 11, 2013
Bruce and I were discussing what the politically correct term is for "little people" and Landon piped in, "I think its munchkins."

February 12, 2013
At Target I was so tempted to take a picture of the line of guys pathetically standing in front of the Valentine's Day cards but then I realized that their ladies will be getting more than I get on Valentine's day. So I didn't.

February 14, 2013
Connor: "I don't have to learn spelling because I'm going to be an artist when I grow up."

February 14, 2013
It's not Valentine's Day until you hear, "Mom, he rubbed my valentine on his butt."

February 18, 2013
Bruce grabbed a bag of 'Pupperoni snacks' and ate 3 of them before he realized it was dog food.

A Mom's Life...in Status Updates

February 21, 2013
Somehow "Honey Bunches of Oats" have been renamed to 'Honey Balls.' So every morning I have to ask, "Who wants Honey Balls?"

February 22, 2013
Landon: "Dixie dog is a good dancer. But make sure you have clothes on when you dance with her because she scratches a lot."

February 24, 2013
Connor: "Are shark's teeth made out of toothpaste?"
Me: "No"
Connor: "So how do sharks brush their teeth?"
Me: "They don't."
Connor: "I wish I was a shark."

February 25, 2013
Landon gave up peanut butter for Lent. Tonight I walked in the kitchen and he had his nose in the jar of peanut butter saying, "I miss this smell."

February 27, 2013
Have you ever waited in line at Subway so long you suddenly get the urge to start popping all the bags of chips?

February 28, 2013
Driving home I saw a huge wild turkey on the road and all I could think was, "And where were you when Pa Ingalls was out hunting for Christmas Dinner?"

March 1, 2013
Landon: "I'm so upset, I feel like saying a word you can't say during Lent!"

March 3, 2013
Evan: "I can fight zombies cuz I eat lots of eggs and I'm strong."

March 4, 2013
I am not one to conform to conventional thoughts. Why bother putting clothes away in dressers or closets when you have a 'laundry' room.

March 5, 2013
I told the boys to eat their supper but Luke responded, "Mom, I don't like ham. I like meat."

March 6, 2013
Me: "So what did you do at school today?"
Luke: "Poop"

March 6, 2013
Random thought from a 10 year old, "Lava and water together would make the perfect hot tub."

March 6, 2013
Suddenly, Connor is afraid of the space between his bed and the wall. He's scared that a hand is going to reach up and grab him. So I literally had to 'talk to the hand' and say, "Hand, Leave Connor Alone!"

March 7, 2013
Evan: "Mom, taco salad is batman food."

March 8, 2013
Everyone was fighting in the car on the way home and 'Math Brain' Landon figured out that Luke was the "greatest common problemator."

March 10, 2013
Lady at the restaurant, "Are you the mom of those FOUR boys?"
Me breaking into a sweat, "yes."
"They are so well behaved."

A Mom's Life...in Status Updates

March 10, 2013
I've decided from now on I will call lunch 'supper' so then I have one less meal to make.

March 11, 2013
Connor comes up with a new excuse every time, "But mom, I can't eat my tator-tot hotdish because it has a force field around it."

March 11, 2013
Tonight's bedtime drama:
"Connor is trying to fart on my pillow."
"Evan is making that gross noise again."
"Mr. Fluffy Pants wrecked by blankets."

March 12, 2013
I was telling the boys that I am going out with the ladies for the weekend and Connor said, "But you are not a lady, you're a mom."

March 17, 2013
I left the drunken Irish in Chicago to return to the rowdy Czechs at home. Both are somewhat annoying, yet always entertaining.

March 18, 2013
Random worry by Landon, "I'm afraid that I will get diabetes and will have to drink orange juice all day."

March 18, 2013
I wonder who is guilty of wrecking Landon's Lego car:
Luke: "Not me!"
Connor: "Not me!"
Evan: "I think it was the invisible guy."

March 19, 2013
Random deep thought: Happiness is being able to fart without consequences.

March 19, 2013
Connor: "How do you get into college?"
Me: "You have to study hard and practice your reading."
Connor: "Why is there going to be a reading race?"

March 20, 2013
Bruce to family: "I'm going to make a phone call, so NO yelling." Thought to self: Have you met this family?

March 22, 2013
Whenever I watch "Cops" I get the urge to practice saying the ABCs backwards and to throw away any white tank tops.

March 23, 2013
It's Saturday and the boys woke up and wanted to do their homework. I think I have entered the twilight zone.

March 23, 2013
Landon colored an Easter egg for Bruce, complete with a butt chin and a bald spot.

March 23, 2013
An elderly couple sat at the table next to us at Culvers and Connor asks (in a not so quiet voice), "Why do some ladies have blue hair?"

March 24, 2013
When Walmart kids go to Target: In the checkout line at Target, Luke opened one of the little beverage coolers and yelled, "Hey mom...do you want a pop? It's FREE!"

March 24, 2013
I was getting the pre-birthday blues until I remembered that birthdays are good for getting free drinks and then I felt better.

A Mom's Life...in Status Updates

March 25, 2013
Landon: "No mom, you cannot be 29 again this year! Can you at least go to 30?"

March 27, 2013
Landon got an iPod and what's the first song he wants to download? A Polka!

March 29, 2013
Luke: "Mom, Connor is saying sentences really loud and swear words really soft!"

March 29, 2013
Landon: "I don't think it's fair that you make us take a bath before we see the doctor and brush our teeth when we see the dentist. I want to be smelly and dirty!"

March 30, 2013
Since last year the boys destroyed their Easter baskets, this year they had to make their own baskets out of paper bags.

March 30, 2013
That awkward moment when paging through a magazine at someone's house and notice that the bookmark is a piece of toilet paper.

March 30, 2013
The boys wanted to leave the Easter Bunny $1.50. But I convinced them it wasn't necessary since he doesn't have any pockets.

March 31, 2013
Me: "Boys put your Easter candy away and let's go to church."
Landon: "Church ruins all the holidays."

April 2, 2013
"Sometimes the toothfairy has way too many teeth to collect in China and can't make it over the ocean before morning. Let's try again tonight."

April 4, 2013
I discovered Dixie was sprayed by a skunk, after she jumped in my bed.

April 5, 2013
Driving in the car this morning:
Evan: "Mom, this needs to stop right now."
Me: "What needs to stop?"
Evan: "Me going to daycare."

April 6, 2013
That awkward moment when you get an impromptu pedicure and then realize you haven't shaved your legs since last fall.

April 7, 2013
Rhyming is now banned in our house...
"I like it when it sprinkles,
My mom has some wrinkles."

April 8, 2013
Connor was a little upset with Bruce and whispered to me, "Can we sell dad and buy a new one?"

April 10, 2013
I was very disturbed when I called home and some strange girl answered. Then I realized it was just Landon.

April 13, 2013
Luke hid all the soap in the house and then said a swear word.

A Mom's Life...in Status Updates

April 13, 2013
That awkward moment when you discover that you are too lazy to run upstairs to get socks but are perfectly fine sitting around with oven mitts on your feet.

April 14, 2013
Landon: "It is so annoying that Evan has no Minecraft abilities!"

April 17, 2013
If there is a show called 'Supper'-nanny, sign me up!

April 21, 2013
Connor was being a trouble maker and then wanted to play the computer. I told him, "No way, not after your antics!" Connor, "WHAT?! I have ants and tics?"

April 21, 2013
For some reason when I hear someone is having twins, I always let out an evil laugh.

April 22, 2013
Luke was crying and holding his leg and I asked what happened. "I was trying to kick Connor and hurt myself."

April 23, 2013
You would think after 10 years he would learn by now.
Me: "Did you brush your teeth?"
Landon: "Did you tell me to?"

April 24, 2013
I guess Luke doesn't like pickles, "Pickles are the son of the devil."

April 26, 2013
I asked Evan if he wanted more meatballs. His response, "No, I burped. So I'm done."

April 28, 2013
According to Evan, he has nine 'smillion' dollars.

April 29, 2013
A little girl at school told me, "One of your Connors was being naughty at school."

May 1, 2013
Luke: "I'm going to get a drink of milk and this time I will use a cup."

May 2, 2013
I've discovered that if I wrap a large ace bandage around my head, the boys will listen to me.

May 2, 2013
So I had a small incident with a clothes hanger and my face. Connor suggested that I ask all my friends to pray for me so I won't have a scar and be ugly forever.

May 3, 2013
Connor: "I think we should get a parrot. So if robbers come we can teach it to say, "Go to the other house. This house doesn't have any money."

May 4, 2013
Landon: "You know how God watches over all of us, it's kind-of like the world's largest Sims game."

May 5, 2013
Connor has a way with the ladies, after the waitress brought him a glass of water he told her, "Thank you, you are a very kind and beautiful girl."

May 6, 2013
Landon's question of the day, "How do you know if you will get a butt chin?"

May 7, 2013
I wonder if mothers of boys have a higher chance of Coors-ism.

A Mom's Life...in Status Updates

May 8, 2013
Connor: "How do birds stand on power lines? Are their feet made of rubber?"

May 9, 2013
Evan: "Dixie is a good dog, she protects the house and when my face is dirty she licks it clean."

May 10, 2013
That annoying moment when you participate in a 'scratch and sniff' ad in the magazine only to find out that it is 'now fragrance free.' It's just embarrassing.

May 10, 2013
Me: "You smell like fart."
Evan: "No, I don't, I brushed my teeth."

May 11, 2013
Evan: "Why did the ants build their ant house on the road?"
Me: "They probably didn't realize it's a road."
Evan: "Why?"
Me: "They don't drive."
Evan: "Why?"
Me: "They don't have tiny cars."
Evan: "Oh."

May 14, 2013
Connor: "I wish I had a 'normal' mom."
Landon: "She's normal, in her own way."

May 15, 2013
Luke: "When I get older I want to have a scar. And eat lots of Pringles."

May 15, 2013
Note to self: No matter how much the kids ask for it: do NOT google image ticks.

May 16, 2013
New house rule: No snuggling until you have a full body tick check.

May 17, 2013
This may be a sign that we eat too much microwavable food around here. We had crock-pot roast beef supper but Connor said, "Ewww, that's old-fashioned food."

May 19, 2013
The Twins lost the baseball game and Landon's explanation was that, "The other team must have practiced."

May 19, 2013
Connor's question of the day, "Did dinosaurs have ticks?"

May 19, 2013
I don't know what is scarier:
-a guy driving down the freeway, holding his mattress on his car
-or me driving down the freeway and trying to take his picture.

May 20, 2013
The first thing Connor said this morning, "Mom, do you remember when I was four and you were a girl zombie?"

May 21, 2013
Question of the day: Does a skid loader leave skid marks?

May 23, 2013
Apparently having a pair of scissors next to a window screen causes one to have "I must cut the screen" tendencies.

May 26, 2013
Evan sat next to the big pack of toilet paper on the way home from the store and he put the seatbelt around it and named it 'Allen.'

A Mom's Life...in Status Updates

May 28, 2013
Connor's observation at the store, "See that guy with the black mustache, he looks like he would have an axe."

May 29, 2013
Enjoying my last 2 hours before school is out for the summer. Not sure if I should take a nap, clean or pack a suitcase.

May 29, 2013
Connor, "Mom, I touched bird poop because I thought it was a rock. So I washed my hands in a mud puddle."

May 29, 2013
Why I love Minnesota: I'm having a sneezing fit at Target and someone a couple aisles down says: "Bless you."

May 30, 2013
Connor decided that if the dentist office had REAL diamond rings for prizes that robbers would go to there every day to get their teeth cleaned.

May 31, 2013
It never fails, I put cleaner in the toilet to "let it soak" and forget about it until someone yells, "Mom the water's blue and I have to pee!"

June 1, 2013
At lunch I had to serve hot-dogs on hamburger buns and Connor said "Mom, I like your new recipe." Yep, mom of the year.

June 1, 2013
Four boys trying to pop bubbles with baseball bats: probably not a good idea.

June 2, 2013
Went to visit Grandpa in the hospital and Evan was trying to push all the elevator buttons with his NOSE!

June 3, 2013
You can tell if Luke is mad at someone, he'll call them a "fat stack of cabbage."

June 4, 2013
Connor: "Is anything possible?"
Me: "Anything can be possible if you put your mind to it."
Connor: "So I can make the earth square?"

June 5, 2013
Playing with Evan and he informed me, "Mom, I'm the boss and you're the minion."

June 6, 2013
You know you're a redneck when your son asks, "Are there people in the world who don't have ticks?"

June 7, 2013
If you're not supposed to cry over spilled milk, what's the protocol for 'thrown milk'?

June 9, 2013
On the way to church Luke says, "Mom, church would be more fun if it had computers and wi-fi."

June 9, 2013
We were asking each other math questions which was all fun until Landon asked, "What is the circumference of a boob?"

June 10, 2013
Landon's question of the day, "Do you know anyone who said "I don't" at a wedding?

June 11, 2013
Out of the blue Luke says, "I wish Supernanny was extinct like the dinosaurs."

June 11, 2013
I butt dialed Poison Control. And yes, I have poison control programmed in my phone, doesn't everybody?

A Mom's Life...in Status Updates

June 12, 2013
Luke: "Mom, Landon got married on Minecraft but now his wife isn't talking to him."

June 13, 2013
You know it's summer when you find freezee wrappers wedged in the couch cushions.

June 16, 2013
Landon: "If someone dared me to eat a whole box of Chicken in a Biskit, I would say, "I accept the challenge."

June 16, 2013
"I bet the toothfairy couldn't come because she had to visit her dad for Father's Day."

June 18, 2013
Random question of the day: "Can girls be allergic to monkeys?"

June 19, 2013
When the Coach wallet arrives at the door, every activity must cease until all the contents are transferred over. Males would never understand this.

June 19, 2013
I really wish Coach made coupon organizers, which probably means I'm more of a Walmart mom than a Coach mom.

June 19, 2013
Landon: "Have you ever watched Jeopardy?"
Me: "Yes"
Landon: "Did you see the one with Neil, a Chinese guy with a blue suit and Doug the really tall guy and some girl?"

June 21, 2013
I've come to the conclusion that it is best for society as a whole that our family resides far out in the country.

June 22, 2013
Me: "I'm going out for my walk now."
Evan: "Can't you take the car so it will be faster?"

June 23, 2013
That awkward moment in church when it smells like fart and you are only surrounded by adults.

June 24, 2013
"Oh shoot, I bet the toothfairy couldn't get in the house last night because I set the security alarm."

June 24, 2013
"Well look at that, the toothfairy left the money under MY pillow. She must have been trying to trick us, silly thing."

June 26, 2013
Luke: "Mom, when I grow up I'm going to build a diamond castle and you can be the mayor."

June 28, 2013
Luke: "Mom, I think you are going to beat the high score of living."

June 29, 2013
Luke handed me my credit card saying, "I can't get this dumb thing to work."

June 30, 2013
Me: "What was your favorite part of the parade?"
Connor: "I liked the Freaky Clown in the huge hamburger."

June 30, 2013
Doing some roleplaying with Landon on what he would do if someone offered him cigarettes or drugs.
Me: "Come on Landon, everyone's doing it. What are you a big chicken or what?"
Landon: "I really like eggs. Did you know that eggs come from chickens?"

A Mom's Life...in Status Updates

July 1, 2013
Words of wisdom by Connor, "If you eat 10 packs of gum a day, your teeth will get rusty."

July 2, 2013
Landon was complaining about swimming lessons, "I don't like doing the 'breath' stroke because I usually run out of air."

July 4, 2013
The boys were sorting through their parade candy and Landon decided that, "A parade is good place for a hobo to get food."

July 7, 2013
Overheard coming from the pool, "Connor you are such an A word! And mom I'm not swearing, it's only a letter."

July 10, 2013
Connor: "Dixie needs to find a boy dog to marry."
Me: "Dogs don't get married."
Connor: "Well, then how do they have babies?"

July 11, 2013
I was upstairs trying to read and warned the boys to be quite saying, "This is my quiet time."
Luke: "So what time is it downstairs?"

July 12, 2013
Connor: "Mom, at swimming lessons I found a fingernail. It was pretty big so I brought it to the lost and found."

July 13, 2013
The boys learned a valuable lesson today: NEVER EVER tell a lady that she has a mustache!

July 14, 2013
Landon just came out of the bathroom with his laptop. There's another multi-tasker in the family.

July 15, 2013
Kayla was disgusted with Evan sticking his foot in the Cheez-It bag. This only means one thing. That she has been gone from home for too long.

July 16, 2013
Connor's new ambition: "When I grow up and am a rich man I'm going make a castle out of Sixlets."

July 18, 2013
Connor: "That's too bad when you get over 10, you can't use your fingers anymore to show how old you are."

July 20, 2013
Evan: "I don't want to go to the parade. It will give me cavities."

July 22, 2013
Connor: "How long do I have to be a twin?"
Me: "Forever, why?"
Connor: "Oh, just wondering."

July 23, 2013
Luke: "Mom remember when we were babies and we slept in a kennel? I liked my kennel."
Me: "I think you mean crib."

July 25, 2013
Tips for playing mini-golf:
1. Do not hit the ball as hard as you can
2. Apologize to the guy that almost got a ball to the head
3. Avoid mini-golf whenever possible

July 25, 2013
The boys were saying their goodbyes to auntie Laura, "Bye Laura! You should go and marry someone. Bye!"

July 26, 2013
I've decided that the bigger the dirty laundry pile, the bigger the reward in heaven.

A Mom's Life...in Status Updates

July 26, 2013
Brought the boys to open savings accounts at the bank.
Connor: "I don't want to sell my money to the bank."
Evan: "I hate the bank! They took all my quarters!"
Luke (to bank teller): "So how much money do you make?"
Landon: "What? I thought I was getting a checkbook."

July 27, 2013
Luke: "Mom, your breath smells like old hotdog water."

July 27, 2013
You know you're a redneck when you bring your boys in for haircuts and are pleasantly surprised when they don't find any ticks.

August 5, 2013
Connor running by, "I'm going to the bathroom, I ate 31 watermelons!"

August 6, 2013
Luke: "Mom can I have a drink of your soda?"
Me: "No, but you can have a drink of pop. P.O.P. We're Minnesotans."

August 6, 2013
We were eating at the Dairy Queen and an ambulance drove by and Landon said, "Maybe they're coming here because someone has brain freeze."

August 7, 2013
At the park, talking to a girl, "My name is Luke. I play the guitar."

August 8, 2013
Connor: "If I had one wish I would wish for a genie that has a robot that mines for gold."

August 9, 2013
What's that old saying, "Friends don't let friends give their kids candy cigarettes?"

August 10, 2013
The first sign you're not at the best China Buffet, "Mom, when I was going to the bathroom some guy puked in the sink."

August 10, 2013
The other sign you're not at the best China Buffet is when all the fortune cookies say the same thing.

September 14, 2013
Our Saturday morning...
1. build an awesome tree fort
2. find a bunny, call it Mr. Whiskers

September 16, 2013
Me: "So how exactly did you lose your frog?"
Luke: "Well, I made it a Lego house and I must have forgot to put a door on it."

September 17, 2013
RIP Mr. Whiskers. It's been a great 3 days.

September 18, 2013
Waiting for the day when the boys will take a shower without me having to tell them, "Don't forget to wash your body and your hair."

September 19, 2013
Connor heading out to the bus, "Bye mom, have a nice 9 hours."

September 19, 2013
Evan: "Mom, if you got attacked by zombies and broke everything in your body, I would take care of you."

September 21, 2013
The son wearing the cross necklace is by far the best behaved. Coincidence or divine intervention?

A Mom's Life...in Status Updates

September 22, 2013
I know it's bedtime for the kids when my eye starts twitching.

September 23, 2013
Forget about being a helicopter parent. I would rather be a blimp: rarely makes an appearance and ready to explode at a moment's notice.

September 24, 2013
Evan: "Mom, I would never put a stinky sock in your face. Never."

September 24, 2013
Me: "A little bloody nose never stopped someone from going to school. The bus is coming, here take this roll of toilet paper with you."

September 25, 2013
The boys were watching a video and I heard a swear word and told them to turn it off. "Mom, it's ok, we didn't learn any new bad words."

September 26, 2013
Luke calls me at work and asks me what his password is for a computer game. Seriously? I can barely remember what year it is.

September 29, 2013
We picked apples from our apple tree and Connor was so surprised, "Mom, taste this! It tastes like a REAL apple."

October 1, 2013
Connor's quote of the day, "When I get in trouble I fart a lot."

October 1, 2013
Luke: "My tastebuds are confused. They only want to eat cheese."

October 2, 2013
We saw some baby twins and Connor said, "I remember when we were born, I told Luke he could go out first."

October 2, 2013
Whenever Evan looks at a calendar and sees the number 2 he insists it's a Tuesday. (Twos-day)

October 4, 2013
Luke to Bruce, "Dad, I will try to pretend that you aren't going bald."

October 6, 2013
How to be passive-aggressive Minnesota style: You post pictures on Facebook and red-eye reduce everyone, except for that ONE person.

October 7, 2013
How far into a corn maze does it take for three out of four boys to realize they have to go pee? About half way.

October 8, 2013
Landon: "Mom, Connor is disrespecting my homework."

October 9, 2013
Presidential trivia by Luke, "Did you know that the president's pet is an eagle? That's why we can't shoot it."

October 10, 2013
We were discussing "who wears the pants in the family" and I looked around and noticed I was the one wearing pants.

October 11, 2013
Landon: I really think it's time that I get a dresser.
Me: Why? You have a perfectly good laundry basket.

October 12, 2013
Landon swept the kitchen, but he left a slice of cheese stuck to the floor because "it wouldn't sweep up."

A Mom's Life...in Status Updates

October 14, 2013
At the China buffet, Connor ate 5 plates of honeydew melon, pats his tummy and says "Oh no, I'm gonna to have the diarrhea tonight."

October 15, 2013
Landon: So what's the deal with Big Foot? Is his other foot normal sized or what?

October 20, 2013
Today I was walking around the house and "sparkly lights" were following me around everywhere! I thought it was a sign that I was a fairy princess. But then realized it was the rhinestones on my butt reflecting the light.

October 21, 2013
Luke: "Mom, I think we should wash the car so people don't think we are dirty."
Me: "Too late."

October 22, 2013
Overheard from the other room: "Sometimes I get watery eyes when I yawn and when I poop."

October 23, 2013
I dug out my red snowflake pajamas and when Connor saw me he said, "Oh mom, I thought you were an elf!"

October 25, 2013
That annoying moment when you have to find something that costs $1.88 in order to qualify for free shipping.

October 26, 2013
Connor noticed that Bruce has chest hairs.
Connor: "Wow, that's a lot of hair."
Bruce: "It's like a rug."
Connor: "A rug with boobs."

October 27, 2013
Bruce yelling from the bathroom..."Tori Spelling annoys me!"
Thought to self: "You messing with my magazines annoys me."

October 28, 2013
Bruce: "Boys get to bed or I'm going to wreak havoc on all of you."
Evan: "What does wreak havoc mean?"
Bruce: "I don't know, it just sounded good."

October 31, 2013
Trick or treating and Bruce's ONE job was to follow us with the vehicle and pick us up when we run out of houses. He lost us. I had to borrow some zombie kid's cell phone to call him.

November 1, 2013
Dear Bruce, You may "think" you are hiding the Halloween candy but it's pretty obvious when you keep coming out of the mudroom chewing. Love, your family

November 4, 2013
The twins are complaining about a homework worksheet and Landon says, "You think that's bad, how would you like to write 20 sentences a week."

November 8, 2013
Connor: "Mom you have a good sense of humor. Can I have more candy?"

November 11, 2013
Morning breath is unhealthy...
Snuggling with Connor this morning, he jumped out of bed and said, "Sorry mom, I really need some healthy air."

A Mom's Life...in Status Updates

November 19, 2013
Landon explaining how he broke his toe:
"Well, I was so happy that I was done writing my President Report and I was running super fast to the computer...and ran into the wall."

November 19, 2013
Landon: "So what's the deal with cereal killers?"

November 20, 2013
Question of the day: "Mom, can pigs dance?"

November 20, 2013
I think I should write a book about all the funny things that the boys say. Good blackmail later in life.

Beware of the levitating, bike riding bad guy.

Connor: "Do you like my picture? It's a waterfall and a dead guy."

A Mom's Life...in Status Updates

Thanks so much for reading!

Coming up in 4-5 years....

A MoM'S LiFe iN StatuS UpdateS: THe TWeeN yearS

Made in the USA
Charleston, SC
27 November 2013